Now may the God of peace himself sanctify you completely, and may your whole spirit and soul and body be kept blameless at the coming of our Lord Jesus Christ. He who calls you is faithful; he will surely do it.

–1 Thessalonians 5:23–24

DAVID BUSH

THE BODY GOSPEL

30 DAYS OF GOSPEL TRUTH THAT WILL TRANSFORM YOUR MIND, BODY & SPIRIT

KING OF KINGS
PUBLISHING

For my mother, Barbara Joyce Bush,
the first author who blazed a trail for a family of authors.
Thank you for always encouraging me,
believing the best about me,
and for giving me permission to dream.

ADVANCE PRAISE FOR
THE BODY GOSPEL

Some books stimulate the mind, some books stir the soul and others move our spirit. David Bush's The Body Gospel is especially important as it speaks to the spirit, soul, and body. You will be impacted in brilliant, surprising and moving ways. If you'll devour this book it will grip your life and, as a result, create a future better than you could imagine. It is a timely and vital message for our generation.

—Gary Wilkerson, President, World Challenge and author of
David Wilkerson: The Cross, The Switchblade, and The Man Who Believed
and *God's Favor: Experiencing The Life God Wants You To Have.*

Contrary to the siren voices sounding at every turn today, your body is not your own. It belongs to God—and doubly so for Christians. God both created us, and then bought us back at the infinite cost of his own Son. He is for the body, and the body is for him. Give David Bush 30 days, just a few minutes each day, to apply Christian theology, in many of its glories, to your perspective, care, and concerns about your body. This is a vital project and pursuit in any age, and especially our day. Don't exercise for mere weight loss, long-term health, or improved physical appearance. Do it to enjoy more of God.

—David Mathis, Executive Editor, desiringGod.org;
Pastor, Cities Church, Minneapolis;
Author, *Habits of Grace: Enjoying Jesus through the Spiritual Disciplines*

Many Christians do not have a clear understanding of how the gospel impacts their pursuit of physical fitness. This book fills the gap—and does an excellent job. There are no superficial, forced, or artificial connections to the gospel here. It is filled with real, helpful, and profound insights on how the gospel should shape and relate to this crucial aspect of our lives. I highly recommend it!

—Matt Perman, Director of Career Development
at The King's College and author of *What's Best Next:
How the Gospel Transforms the Way You Get Things Done*

David Bush is a voice crying out in the 'Wilderness of the Unwell' saying, "Prepare ye the way of the Lord!"

This 30-day, Scripture-laden devotional has the substance to create a paradigm shift which will enable you to align your heart and mind with the heart and mind of Jesus. David's guidance will lead you to truly grasp the importance of the stewardship of your body, so you will be able to fully love God with all your heart, mind, soul and STRENGTH!

—Lisa Morrone, P.T., and author of *Get Healthy for Heaven's Sake*

I firmly believe there is an undeniable connection between physical body stewardship and spiritual Body ministry. David Bush's The Body Gospel challenges every follower of Christ to examine their motivations, habits and physical disciplines in light of the truth of God's Word. Be forewarned: if followed for 30 days, it will force you to grapple with a significant number of uncomfortable issues. Read. Ponder. Apply.

—J. Paul Nyquist, Ph.D.
Vice President of Discipleship, College of Biblical Studies and Author of *Prepare*

Being a broadcaster and therefore in the public eye, many people come to me asking for guidance in losing weight after I lost 100 pounds. There are many reasons people want to lose weight, many of which can actually be more destructive than helpful. David Bush is absolutely right—you should know exactly why you have such a desire, then dare to ask yourself how that fits in with glorifying God rather than yourself. After all, He made you. Without Him there would be no you. What percentage do you owe to Him? That's easy…100%. And that's even BEFORE you hear the magnificent salvation story. Thank you David for getting this right and helping people build on solid rock rather than shifting sand!

—Van Harden, Marconi Award-winning broadcaster and Author of
How You Look and How You Feel and *Life In The Purple Wedge*

Your eyes saw my unformed substance; in your book were written, every one of them, the days that were formed for me, when as yet there was none of them.

—Psalm 139:16

AUTHOR
ACKNOWLEDGEMENT

Many people are responsible for helping this book idea become a reality.

Significant editorial assistance was provided by Stephen and Alison Bush, Julie Summa, and Michael Mudlaff. I am most appreciative of their concern for biblical orthodoxy and attention to detail.

Thanks to Gregg Stearns and Becky Johnson for their help in formatting the principles I wanted to communicate.

Thanks to many prayer partners who have held this project up before the Lord.

Thanks to my wife, Beth, and family who have made sacrifices and brought encouragement throughout the process of writing and publishing this book.

Soli Deo Gloria
David Bush
September, 2019

INSIDE

Introduction by
David Bush

Before you step on the treadmill, join the local health club, or take the latest diet craze for a test drive, let me ask you a question: Why are you doing this? Considering the failure rate fitness seekers are experiencing today, this is not an irrelevant question. Your motivation and rationale for losing weight, building muscle mass, or accomplishing an athletic feat is critically important and will have an oversized impact on your ultimate success.

Another equally important question every Christ follower needs to ask is, "How should the gospel influence my goal-setting and approach to the task?" Despite understanding the need to integrate biblical thinking into the many facets of their lives, many Christians have no clear connection between their faith and their pursuit of physical fitness.

"What's the gospel got to do with exercise and fitness?" you ask. "The gospel is important for saving people from their sins, not burpees and bench presses!" "After all, the Bible is a book about stewarding our spiritual lives, not physical transformation…right?"

Questions and perspectives like these reveal a core

problem: Many don't recognize the fact that the gospel touches every aspect of their lives, including the care and disciplining of their physical bodies. God's provision of redemption, salvation, and wholeness by faith alone, through grace alone, and in Christ alone makes all the difference in forming the why that will sustain any pursuit of healthy living.

In regard to your physical state, have you become a slave to the kind of short-term thinking so prevalent in our culture: What will get me that job? What will get me that date? What will get me into that pair of jeans?

Has your approach to health become centered on you? What will get me noticed? What will postpone that procedure? What will lower my medical premium? What will help me feel better?

The seeming inability to consistently discipline ourselves physically, along with our self-centered approach, has led our North American culture to an illogical impasse. At the same time we have more information, programs, and facilities to ensure good health, we are experiencing an unprecedented explosion in chronic, lifestyle diseases that are limiting the productivity and longevity of a large swath of the population. Tragically, it is also compromising the witness and effectiveness of the church.

Many Christians have a nagging sense they could do better with body care, a belief that is backed up by statistics showing the church is less healthy than the unhealthy culture that surrounds it. At the same time, we also reject the self-centered and narcissistic rationales for better health that our culture is serving up. We rightly reject these motives for investing in our health, all while a nagging sense of missed opportunity clings to us like the extra weight we would like to lose.

Clearly, our tools, systems, methodologies, information, and incentives for maintaining a satisfactory level of health are lacking something. Without an alternative, Christians tend to adopt contemporary strategies to fitness and experience the same uninspiring results.

We have tried things the world's way, complete with physical objectification, unworthy goals, and narcissistic impulses. Perhaps it is time to try a different approach when formulating our motives for better body care.

Enter the gospel.

I believe the Creator of our bodies has something valuable to say regarding our stewardship of them. The gospel is, as with all of life, central to this message. After all, God has the most at stake as it is His investment, and the ultimate productivity of it, that is on the line. In light of this, He has provided counsel, direction, and gospel truth He wants us to apply in this key sphere of life.

I invite you to invest 30 days considering biblical motivations for good body stewardship and receive encouragement for a lifelong pursuit of health. A pursuit whose goal is maximum availability to accomplish what God has said is of primary importance: loving, serving, and glorifying Him and serving others completely and effectively. As is the case in all things, I believe you will find that God's motives for body stewardship are wholly superior and more satisfying than anything the world offers.

At the core of this pursuit of a worthy why is the gospel. Its message regarding God, man, Jesus, and eternity is as relevant to your journey of sanctification as it was to your salvation. The gospel that saved you is the same gospel that continues to sanctify and transform you for God's glory.

THE BODY GOSPEL holds the potential to free you from the self-serving paradigms of a self-centered world. It provides a blueprint for building a lasting, lifelong pursuit of physical availability to both reflect the image of your Creator and accomplish everything He has purposed for you in His sovereignty.

Why take on the inconvenience and effort involved in pursuing a healthy, available life? I pray you will find the answer to that important question as you let God's word inform your thinking, mold your motivations and animate your action.

I Was Created By God Uniquely, Purposefully, And Lovingly.

ENGAGE…a New Day

A loving God created my body, soul, and spirit on purpose and for a purpose. This fact alone gives my life great significance. At my birth I possessed unique physical characteristics that sprang from His creative genius, which pleased Him, and which hold the potential to bring glory to God and serve His eternal purposes.

DAY 1

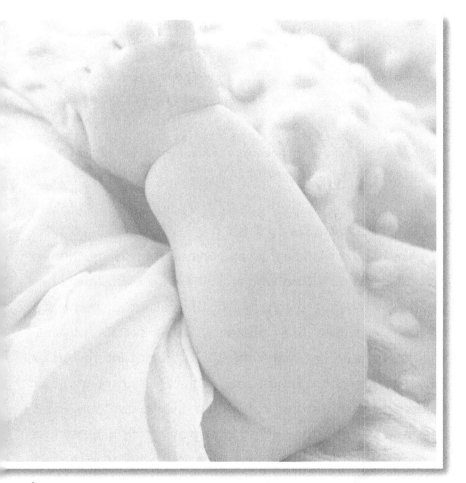

ELEVATE...with God's Word

For you formed my inward parts; you knitted me together in my mother's womb.

I praise you, for I am fearfully and wonderfully made. Wonderful are your works; my soul knows it very well. My frame was not hidden from you, when I was being made in secret, intricately woven in the depths of the earth. Your eyes saw my unformed substance; in your book were written, every one of them, the days that were formed for me, when as yet there was none of them.

—Psalm 139:13–16

Before I formed you in the womb I knew you, and before you were born I consecrated you; I appointed you a prophet to the nations.

—Jeremiah 1:5

For we are his workmanship, created in Christ Jesus for good works, which God prepared beforehand, that we should walk in them.

—Ephesians 2:10

Why, even the hairs of your head are all numbered. Fear not; you are of more value than many sparrows.

—Luke 12:7

EXCHANGE...with David Bush

Just like trillions of individual and unique snowflakes, there is no one like you. A God who is limitless in His creativity has clearly demonstrated this fact in the collage of humanity. While our culture may presently value certain physical characteristics more than others, God is not interested or influenced by these judgments. Different skin colors, hair colors and textures, eye colors, hip and lip contours, gum lines and belly buttons—God is displaying His majesty in a myriad of ways! Your worth and value are anchored in the fact you are God's purposeful creation who bears His image.

There is not one body type that brings Him more glory than another, but several God-designed body types that equally delight Him. Three well-accepted categorizations are ectomorph, mesomorph, and endomorph. Each has characteristics that favor certain types of activities and possess different levels of strength and endurance, and all can achieve a healthy height-to-weight ratio.

Let's be honest. There will be a natural pull to be culturally relevant in our appearance, as well as a tendency to dislike aspects of our God-designed base model. I always felt blessed to have received the color of eyes I have, and I have received many compliments on them throughout my life. My hairline, however, has seemed to me more of a bane than a blessing. I also naturally have hair all over my body that prompted my father to call me "Daveman the Caveman." Because of this, I have received many ribbings over the years, including oft-repeated comments from my father-in-law who says, "You have a marketing problem, Dave. Good production but poor distribution." Needless to say, nearly everyone can find something to appreciate about what God made as well as something that must be accepted with grace.

It is clear from our scripture passages that God had a purposeful vision for each of us that had implications for our physical body and its ability to accomplish a predetermined agenda for our lives. An appropriate question for all of us to ask our Creator is, "How can I cooperate with Your vision for my physical state in order to maximize my ability to glorify You and serve others?" In other words, what is the best godly version of me God had in mind when I sprang from His creative genius?

Our culture can become fixated on hairstyles, hemlines, bustlines, and body ink, but God is more concerned with functionality. Can I accept how He created me (this may well be different than what I have become through my behaviors), take joy in the fact that He found it acceptable, and commit myself to maximize the beauty and vitality I possess as a response to His love and grace?

Notes:

EXPLORE...a Fresh Start

1. Have you ever thought deeply about the implications of the fact that you were God's intentional creation?

2. Can you find the references to your body, soul, and spirit in Psalm 139 and Ephesians 2?

3. Are you angry about any part of how He designed your physical being?

4. What aspects of your current physical state are a result of God's creation (things you could never control), and what aspects show the influence of your decisions, behavior, and lifestyle choices?

5. Does the fact that God was pleased with how He originally created you help to silence the critics who are quick to point out "flaws" with your body type and unique physical characteristics—including the critic in your own head?

ENJOY...a New You!

You are unique and loved by your Creator. He has given you the ability to glorify Him by pursuing His vision for your physical body!

Pursuing God's purpose and plan,

My Value And Identity Are Found And Are Secure In Christ.

ENGAGE...a New Day

While the pursuit of better health or a more balanced life will almost certainly produce greater vitality, clarity of mind, and spiritual endurance, no physical state or goal achieved will change a thing about my inestimable value to God. My identity as a believer is and must always be founded on who I am in Christ.

ELEVATE...with God's Word

...he has now reconciled in his body of flesh by his death, in order to present you holy and blameless and above reproach before him,

—Colossians 1:22

For I am sure that neither death nor life, nor angels nor rulers, nor things present nor things to come, nor powers, nor height nor depth, nor anything else in all creation, will be able to separate us from the love of God in Christ Jesus our Lord.

—Romans 8:38-39

And it is God who establishes us with you in Christ, and has anointed us, and who has also put his seal on us and given us his Spirit in our hearts as a guarantee.

—2 Corinthians 1:21-22

But God, being rich in mercy, because of the great love with which he loved us, even when we were dead in our trespasses, made us alive together with Christ—by grace you have been saved—and raised us up with him and seated us with him in the heavenly places in Christ Jesus, so that in the coming ages he might show the immeasurable riches of his grace in kindness toward us in Christ Jesus.

—Ephesians 2:4-7

EXCHANGE…with David Bush

Identity theft has become a major concern in recent years as technology, mobility, and convenience have conspired to reduce our identity to a series of numbers that can easily be confiscated by others with nefarious motives. Many people wake to find that credit cards, car leases, and even home mortgages have been secured by strangers in their name. A number of services are now available that will help to protect your identity and spare you the lost time, frustration, and ruined credit that identity theft can inflict.

Identity theft is even more prevalent outside the world of banking and credit. In fact, for many believers, identity theft has become a daily state of existence. A secure value and identity that was bought for us by Christ has been compromised by a culture that is interested only in conformation to its values and tastes.

When you think about your value, do you instinctively think about what you can do or tasks you can perform for others? When you think about your identity, do you think about an image you wish to project or a group to which you belong? While it is common to think about ourselves this way, the gospel frees us from an identity shaped by what we do to one that is fundamentally about whose we are.

We have been bought out of the slave market of sin and adopted into Christ's family, with all the privileges and rights this affords (this is what the term redemption means in Ephesians 1:7). While all people have intrinsic value to God because He created them in His image, those who have placed their faith in Jesus have been adopted into His family and share in a new identity. Gone is the shame, condemnation, and unworthiness that formerly molded our thinking; now replaced by freedom, worthiness, and significance because we are viewed as being in Christ. God thinks His Son Jesus is the best, and because we now share His identity as His followers, God sees us the same way. He no sooner would reject us than He would His own Son.

This extraordinary news about our value and identity should be a game-changer in the area of body care and self-image. For starters, the culture does not define our value anymore—God does; and as we have seen, He thinks His kids are awesome! We do not have to conform to some cultural ideal, as God is pleased with how He made us. He has given us His Holy Spirit to both assure us He is not trading us in for something better, as well as to assist us in our transformation to Christlikeness. In a world where nothing seems certain and today's hot property is tomorrow's afterthought, we have security in knowing our value and identity is rooted in Someone who possesses ultimate, eternal significance.

Hopefully, your physical body will increasingly reflect the reality of whose you are. Regardless of whether that alignment is currently taking place, your identity as a son or daughter of God is an eternal reality purposefully designed to motivate, encourage, and inspire you.

Notes:

EXPLORE...a Fresh Start

1. What are the roots of a poor self-image? Comparison? Ignorance? Valuing other's opinions over God's?

2. What would change in your perspective of body care if you sincerely believed God loved and viewed you like He does His Son Jesus?

3. Does truth like this cause you to want to "let yourself go" physically (after all, nothing will change my identity) or "up your game" (What steps can I take to transform my life to my true identity)?

ENJOY...a New You!

Your value will never be based on what you can do for God. In Christ, you perfectly please your Heavenly Father!

Enjoying the security of being in Christ,

My Thoughts About My Body Must Always Be Informed By Gospel Truth.

ENGAGE...a New Day

Whether or not my body currently aligns with God's intentions for me does not change the fact that I am unconditionally loved by Him. While the Spirit may provoke me to change my behavior and direction in the physical sphere, He will always want me to be motivated by love for God and others,

DAY 3

gratitude, and grace. God does not use shame and self-loathing to accomplish His purposes; in fact, these are Satan's tools and are counterproductive to transformation.

ELEVATE...with God's Word

For all who are led by the Spirit of God are sons of God. For you did not receive the spirit of slavery to fall back into fear, but you have received the Spirit of adoption as sons, by whom we cry, "Abba! Father!" The Spirit himself bears witness with our spirit that we are children of God.

—Romans 8: 14-16

See what kind of love the Father has given to us, that we should be called children of God; and so we are.

—1 John 3:1a

For the love of Christ controls us, because we have concluded this: that one has died for all, therefore all have died; and he died for all, that those who live might no longer live for themselves but for him who for their sake died and was raised

—2 Corinthians 5:14

For by grace you have been saved through faith. And this is not your own doing; it is the gift of God, not a result of works, so that no one may boast.

—Ephesians 2:8-9

EXCHANGE...with David Bush

My personal interactions with Christians regarding their state of health tend to follow a predictable script. The first words out of their mouths are often of a self-deprecating, confessional nature. "I'm kinda embarrassed by what's happened to me." "You'd never guess I was voted Prom Queen in high school." "I haven't always looked like this." I often see in their eyes a sense of hopelessness and a certainty that they are disappointing God and others they care about.

Most Christians know they are not as healthy as they

should be. If you are carrying significantly more weight than is healthy, it is almost certain you are aware of this fact, and it is possible the shame and sense that you are disappointing God and others fuels a sense of unworthiness that keeps you stuck there. If only you could do better, you think, you would be more deserving of God's love, grace, and favor.

While this way of thinking is common, we need to remember that God has never been particularly impressed with our behavior, and it wasn't why He saved us in the first place. The gospel saves us from having to "get our act together" before we can have a relationship with God. The fact is, none of us ever did or ever will have our act together. The gospel that liberated us from our sin apart from our works is the same gospel that continues to liberate us daily as we fall short of God's standard.

Despite an acknowledgement of God's grace toward us, it is not uncommon for those who know Jesus to despair over their physical condition. For many believers, this seems to be one area of sanctification that consistently remains just outside of the Spirit's redemptive process.

Where this situation exists, it is critical that we not adopt a performance-based mentality that equates conformity to God's standard with acceptance by Him. Attempting to earn God's love or favor through the pursuit of health or some athletic accomplishment misrepresents the core of the gospel. God doesn't accept us on our own merits, but Christ's. God loves His Son, and when He sees His Son in us, He is perfectly pleased, regardless of the kind of physical condition we're in.

God absolutely desires our obedience, including the way we steward our physical bodies. He wants us to be motivated to obey Him and steward our bodies because of our love for Him and others, and gratitude for the stewardship He has entrusted to us. He seeks to motivate us with the Greatest Commandment (loving others as we love ourselves), rather than the motivational tools of the world that trade in guilt, shame, and attempts to earn approval.

Could it be that the gospel is the answer to your body care struggle? The answer is almost certainly "yes." The dysfunction we exhibit in various areas of our lives is rooted in the misunderstanding or misappropriation of the glorious truth and grace of the gospel, which is stated so beautifully by the Apostle Paul in Roman 8:1–4 (ESV):

Therefore, there is now no condemnation for those who are in Christ Jesus, because through Christ Jesus the law of the Spirit who gives life has set you free from the law of sin and death. For what the law was powerless to do because it was weakened by the flesh, God did by sending his own Son in the likeness of sinful flesh to be a sin offering. And so he condemned sin in the flesh, in order that the righteous requirement of the law might be fully met in us, who do not live according to the flesh but according to the Spirit.

EXPLORE...a Fresh Start

1. Do you think God loves you right now...or is He waiting for something to change before He can love you?

2. Guilt and shame are powerful motivators. What in your life is motivated by them?

3. Romans 8:1–4 speaks to the fact that we are powerless to affect change in our lives because of the weakness of our flesh. What gospel strategy for change does Paul commend to us?

4. God desires your obedience...but by what does He want your obedience to be motivated?

ENJOY...a New You!

Isn't it wonderful to know God provokes change through the good news of the gospel? In the midst of a culture of lies, God speaks the truth!

Walking with you in the grace and truth of the gospel,

God Owns And Is In Charge Of My Body.

ENGAGE...a New Day

The Creator has the right to claim authority over whatever He creates, and God exercises this right by laying claim to my physical body. Furthermore, followers of Jesus surrender themselves to the authority of the One who bought them out of slavery to sin and rebellion. If I am married, the best I can claim is "third dibs" on body ownership, as my spouse is to have greater authority.

ELEVATE...with God's Word

Do you not know that your bodies are members of Christ?...You are not your own, for you were bought with a price. So glorify God in your body.

—1 Corinthians 6:15a,19b-20

The earth is the Lord's and the fullness thereof, the world and those who dwell therein.

—Psalm 24:1

For none of us lives to himself, and none of us dies to himself. For if we live, we live to the Lord, and if we die, we die to the Lord. So then, whether we live or whether we die, we are the Lord's.

—Romans 14:7-8

...as it is my eager expectation and hope that I will not be at all ashamed, but that with full courage now as always Christ will be honored in my body, whether by life or by death. For to me to live is Christ, and to die is gain.

—Philippians 1:20-21

For the wife does not have authority over her own body, but the husband does. Likewise the husband does not have authority over his own body, but the wife does.

—1 Corinthians 7:4

EXCHANGE...with David Bush

Growing up, it was not unusual for me to eat at McDonald's restaurants. Even as a kid more interested in a Big Mac®, fries, and a shake than historical propaganda, I remember seeing plaques at every location lauding "Founder" Ray Kroc as an innovative and benevolent businessman. It wasn't until a couple of years ago I learned that Kroc wasn't the original owner of McDonald's, but that he purchased it for a little over two million dollars from the original owners in 1961.

Most people have also learned in recent years that Mark Zuckerberg wasn't the originator of Facebook, but that the Winklevoss twins actually created the idea first.

In both of these examples, the original owners found out that new ownership brought with it uncomfortable, often ego-shattering realities. From corporate culture to business strategy to recipes, things change when a new sheriff is in town. Kroc even opened a competing McDonald's restaurant across the street from the original McDonald brothers' restaurant in San Bernardino, California, eventually driving it out of business.

While the ruthlessness and motives of the new owners in these examples I've cited are not commendable, the principle should not be lost. New ownership means surrendering rights that were formerly held.

A broad misunderstanding of this principle of ownership exists when it comes to our physical bodies. While God had the right to ownership of your body as your Creator, the indwelling presence of the Holy Spirit represents the title deed and removes any speculation in the matter. First Corinthians chapter six (among other verses) makes it clear that God's authority over our being is not relegated to the spiritual aspects of our lives; he is the owner of our physical bodies as well. Our role as former owners is to comply with the directives of the new owner, regardless of how we preferred to run our business before the transfer of ownership.

For all of us, this can be a hard truth to come to terms with, as we prefer to operate more as *franchisees* than *corporate-owned stores.*The news for married folks is even more challenging, as we learn in 1 Corinthians 7 that our spouses have greater rights over our bodies than we do! Husbands, have your wives asked you to consider changes in your eating habits or shown concern about your weight? How about your habit of riding a motorcycle without a helmet? Wives, have your husbands expressed concern about a medication you're taking or voiced frustration about the frequency of intimacy? We all bristle at requested changes to behavior when we're living under the false and unbiblical assumption that we get to make the decisions regarding our bodies.

While new ownership of a business may bring about a mixed bag of success or failure, our cooperation with God's ownership of our bodies will always result in positive transformation. As was the case with McDonald's and Facebook, it should be our goal to remove the fingerprints of our "ownership" so that observers will assume God was the Founder.

EXPLORE...a Fresh Start

1. What kind of response does the realization that God owns the rights to your body bring? Have you ever considered that this is a part of what submitting to the Lordship of Christ means?

2. How would you discover what expectations God has of your body that He owns? How can this devotional help in that regard?

3. Have you ever rented a home to someone else...Allowed someone to borrow clothes or equipment that belonged to you...Let someone stay at your vacation home? What were your expectations regarding how they treated your property?

4. What pressures, burdens, and responsibilities are borne by owners versus those that are borne by renters or employees? What ownership responsibilities have you assumed that God did not intend for you to have?

ENJOY...a New You!

Surrendering ownership brings freedom and joy! You don't have to carry the burden or suffer from the mistakes of mismanagement that being an "owner-operator" brings.

Surrendering control daily to the true Owner,

God Is Sovereign Over My Lifespan.

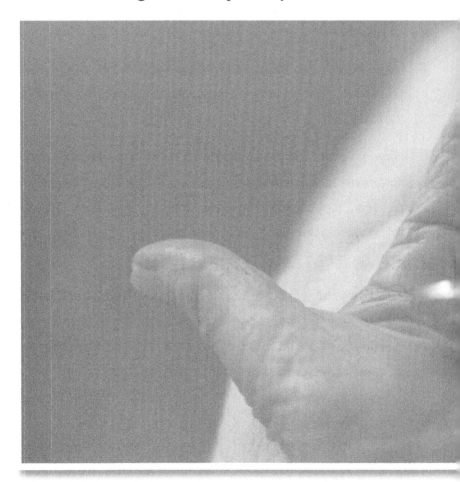

ENGAGE...a New Day

God's sovereignty and my personal responsibility are always in tension. While my wise body stewardship will impact the effectiveness and productivity of the years God gives me, I do not ultimately control the length of my days. My goal should be to maximize my effectiveness, not control my destiny.

DAY 5

ELEVATE...with God's Word

Since his days are determined, and the number of his months is with you, and you have appointed his limits that he cannot pass.

—Job 14:5

And which of you by being anxious can add a single hour to his span of life?

—Matthew 6:27

Your eyes saw my unformed substance; in your book were written, every one of them, the days that were formed for me, when as yet there was none of them.

—Psalm 139:16

And I will say to my soul, "Soul, you have ample goods laid up for many years; relax, eat, drink, be merry."' But God said to him, 'Fool! This night your soul is required of you, and the things you have prepared, whose will they be?' So is the one who lays up treasure for himself and is not rich toward God."

—Luke 12:19-21

EXCHANGE...with David Bush

A note recently found in a car that had been traded in to a dealership sparked universal condemnation. The checklist of 22 *demands* a girl was making of her boyfriend went viral when it was shared on social media. The bizarre list detailed what she expected from her boyfriend in regard to his friends, other women, and the way she would like to be treated. It included expectations that she would receive replies to her texts within ten minutes, that he would tell her he loved her at least once a day, and that he couldn't spend time with his friends more than twice a week.

This poor guy received the pity of all men and most women. It epitomized the kinds of demands someone makes when they are a *control freak.*

It's interesting how we, in our relationship to God, can manifest some of these same tendencies. We often adopt a quid pro quo mindset that places expectations on God for our good behavior. "I'm behaving well, so God is obligated to provide me _____." In short, we start to think we can control outcomes, and we often find Scripture that seems to support this notion. The Proverbs of Solomon are fertile ground for verses that seem to ensure outcomes when we act wisely. In these cases, it's important to remember that Solomon's proverbs are general principles, not absolute promises.

We need to be careful in our approach to our body care in this area. When we think God must grant us a long and healthy life because of our physical discipline, we risk becoming prideful. Scripture clearly teaches God is sovereign, and He is in charge of our lifespan, not us. We all know people who have cared well for themselves who have died relatively young, as well as those who have abused their bodies and lived into their 90s.

In light of this reality, do we live fatalistically and say, "I can't change my lifespan, so I might as well live as I please?" Of course not. This line of thinking is the same as the person who says we don't ever need to share our faith because God is going to call everyone He wants to save to Himself without us. God does call people to faith, but He's chosen to use us in the process.

This entire devotional is filled with biblical admonitions and gospel-centered reasons why we should pursue healthy lifestyle habits. I'm doing this in spite of the fact that God already knows our lifespan. Among the lessons we're learning are the benefits of an energetic life, God's goal of transformation, His expectation of wise stewardship, and the necessity of loving God completely and serving others.

God knows the number of our days, but we don't. In the midst of that mystery, let's commit to putting nothing in the way of serving and honoring Him and others. Personally, I'm going to live like my actions are of consequence while simultaneously acknowledging God's sovereignty.

Notes:

EXPLORE…a Fresh Start

1. How might a person's pursuit of a healthy lifestyle actually be motivated by fear?

2. How does resting in God's sovereignty bring peace and perspective to our body care?

3. How does God's sovereignty allow us to rightly focus our body stewardship efforts? Would our belief in His sovereignty change our approach to some medical procedures?

ENJOY...a New You!

Your lifespan is in God's capable hands! In the midst of God's sovereignty, you are still given freedom to make choices that can bless God, yourself, and others.

Yours for the journey,

The Culture Will Consistently Provide Bad Ideas, Impure Motives, Unworthy Goals, And Outright Lies Regarding My Health And My Body.

ENGAGE...a New Day

The culture offers endless ideas and opinions regarding how I should view and treat my physical body. These views, summarized in the statement, "It's my body, and I'll do what I want with it", are manifested in behavior that alternately obsesses and pampers or disfigures and degrades my body.

DAY 6

ELEVATE...with God's Word

Do not be conformed to this world, but be transformed by the renewal of your mind, that by testing you may discern what is the will of God, what is good and acceptable and perfect

—Romans 12:2

For all that is in the world—the desires of the flesh and the desires of the eyes and pride of life—is not from the Father but is from the world.

—1 John 2:16

See to it that no one takes you captive by philosophy and empty deceit, according to human tradition, according to the elemental spirits of the world, and not according to Christ.

—Colossians 2:8

EXCHANGE...with David Bush

In high school wrestling I sometimes had to resort to extreme measures to make weight. One time in particular stands out, when my first misadventure with suppositories produced a rather untimely and embarrassing result! As Forest Gump famously stated, "That's all I'm going to say about that." In my immaturity, I didn't see that this and other culturally acceptable bad ideas regarding weight loss could exact a cost.

There are people who will lose weight purely out of a desire to conform to a cultural ideal, to extract compliments or attention on social media, or to show their ex what they're missing. These kinds of accomplishments, often cheered on by a peer group, are driven by impure motives.

I know one brother in Christ who has made it his life goal to run a marathon in every state in the union. I can't begin to estimate the time and money this will consume, in addition to the toll this will take on his feet and joints.

Bad ideas, impure motives, and unworthy goals prevail in the arena of health and body care. These man-centered, often narcissistic perspectives usually focus on personal performance and appearance and can place us in bondage to life-controlling substances or routines.

In his letter to the Roman church, the Apostle Paul identifies the root from which our culture's schizophrenic views of the body grows:

Claiming to be wise, they became fools, and exchanged the glory of the immortal God for images resembling mortal man and birds and animals and creeping things.

Therefore God gave them up in the lusts of their hearts to impurity, to the dishonoring of their bodies among themselves, because they exchanged the truth about God for a lie and worshiped and served the creature rather than the Creator, who is blessed forever! Amen. Romans 1:24–25 (ESV)

This is the epicenter of the perspective that ruled Rome and currently rules our culture as well. The results have been catastrophic. It is impossible to navigate a straight course when your moral compass does not recognize true north.

Christians are not immune to the wrong-headed thinking about our bodies that has taken so many captive. We gain ultimate Truth in God's Word and possess an internal compass courtesy of the Holy Spirit. Yet followers of Christ appear to be just as prone to both broad indifference and false messages about health and fitness as those who are left to their own darkened thinking.

When we seek biblical wisdom for our health journey, we will see with greater clarity issues that have confused us. We will see the obvious shortcomings of rapid weight loss. We will not become suckers for health and diet scams that promise easy results. We will not do damage to our bodies in an attempt to impress others or align with some arbitrary cultural ideal. Where we have not been thinking rightly about our bodies, we can repent and seek God's help in aligning our thinking with His.

Our godless culture has a source for many of its directives regarding our bodies: the Devil. Let's not forget Satan's end game for us all: he wants us dead, and the sooner the better. This was his agenda in the Garden of Eden with Adam and Eve, and it hasn't changed. Whether it's years of compromised effectiveness in the life of a Christ-follower, or an unbeliever's fit of despair that ends in suicide, death and ruination are the goals. For the prince of this world, it doesn't matter if our health is compromised (or death comes) as a result of alcoholism, cancer from tobacco use, illicit drugs, anabolic steroids, sexual misconduct, or chronic disease.

We need spiritual discernment to filter the information we receive regarding our bodies and our health. Discernment begins with the understanding that this world—and the spiritual forces driving it—are not our friends. As with so many areas of our lives, it will feel like a daily struggle to swim against the current. But as you will see as we progress, we have been given every resource necessary to successfully persevere in the journey!

EXPLORE...a Fresh Start

1. In your health journey, what have you tried that turned out to be a bad idea? How does the world capitalize on those who wish to change their appearance?

2. What motives have you had in the past for pursuing better health? Can you identify your current motivation?

3. How might you determine if a health goal is worthy or unworthy?

4. Do you see God's Word as a source for wisdom for all of life—or just certain topics?

ENJOY...a New You!

God's Word is sufficient to guide our thinking in the area of health and fitness! God does not leave us without biblical wisdom in one of the most important areas of our lives.

Trying to walk wisely in a confused culture,

My Bodily Discipline Will Have A Direct Impact On My Ability To Fulfill The Great Commandment To Love God With All My Heart, Soul, Mind, And Strength.

ENGAGE...a New Day

Loving God with all I am has implications for my physical body. The practical outcomes of my love will, by necessity, include my ability to worship Him, obey Him, and make His priorities my priorities. To the degree that my life choices present physical obstacles to loving Him, I need to reorient my habits and behaviors to those which free me to love Him completely.

ELEVATE...with God's Word

And you shall love the Lord your God with all your heart and with all your soul and with all your mind and with all your strength.

—Mark 12:30

I appeal to you therefore, brothers, by the mercies of God, to present your bodies as a living sacrifice, holy and acceptable to God, which is your spiritual worship.

—Romans 12:1

For God has not given us a spirit of timidity, but of power and love and discipline.

—2 Timothy 1:7 (NASB)

If you love me, keep my commandments.

—John 14:15

EXCHANGE…with David Bush

For many people, the Great Commandment evokes pictures of passionate worship, giving voice to our love for and devotion to our Creator. The real test of our ability to fulfill this commandment, however, usually takes place in the day-to-day ruminations and routines of our lives.

Loving God with your heart, soul, mind, and strength is, at its core, the pursuit of a disciplined life. It's what makes the foundational command of the Bible so challenging. Few of us naturally gravitate toward discipline, whether it is our sleeping schedule, our prayer and devotional life, our eating and exercise habits, or our ability to control our tongue. My life has been a long, slow journey of learning discipline in my eating and exercise habits, my financial life, my prayer and devotional life, my sexual life, my thought life, and many other areas. I am still a work in progress. Discipline means consistently denying ourselves something that might seem easier or more pleasurable. Only through consistency and perseverance are disciplines established in our lives.

Loving God with all your heart means setting your affections on the things He loves and values. Hating sin and pursuing righteousness are good indications you are loving God with all your heart. These are put to the test when you are drawn to love the things, the influence, and the respect of this world.

Loving God with all your soul means serving God passionately with the gifts, talents, and opportunities He has presented to you. It means abandoning your agenda to serve Him fully. We are tested daily with both the desire to take credit for our abilities as well as to seek ways to serve ourselves.

Loving God with all your mind means conforming your thoughts to what is true and what God has revealed about Himself in His Word. It includes developing your mental capacity and offering it to Him for His use and glory. Constantly seeking amusement and entertainment, not seeking to reach our potential academically, and exposing ourselves to impure words and images makes loving God with our mind impossible.

Loving God with all your strength means developing and protecting your physical capacity so as to live vitally and accomplish all He desires with you, for as long as He desires you to live. A sedentary lifestyle, poor nutrition choices, and a lack of concern regarding how God might want to use your physical capacity work against loving God in this way.

None of these ways of loving God come naturally to us. They all require discipline. And, as the Old Testament followers of the Law discovered, they are impossible without the intervention and assistance of the Holy Spirit. We won't deny ourselves in order to give more to God without the Holy Spirit birthing a vision in us for how worthy He is to receive that kind of devotion.

In a church culture that is, according to studies, ten percent more unhealthy than an unhealthy culture at large, it's hard to see how we are loving God with all our strength. This appears to be an area we can grow in, especially when we realize how deficits in this area can easily impact our ability to love well in other areas.

Notes:

EXPLORE...a Fresh Start

1. With what love command do you find it easiest to discipline yourself? Which is most difficult?

2. Have you thought about loving God as more than an emotional response or expression?

3. How can you tangibly love God with all your strength in the days ahead?

Mark 12: 30

LOVE
the Lord your
GOD
with all your *Heart*
with all your Soul
with all your *MIND*
with all your **strength**

ENJOY...a New You!

Find a new perspective on how you can love God. You can express your love for God today and every day by getting adequate rest, drinking more water, ditching the empty calories and going for a brisk walk.

Seeking to love God completely,

My Bodily Discipline Will Have A Direct Impact On My Ability To Fulfill The Great Commandment To Love My Neighbor As Myself.

ENGAGE...a New Day

I am commanded to love my neighbors as I love myself. My closest neighbors include my spouse and/or family, and expands to my physical neighbors, co-workers, fellow believers, community and world. I cannot tangibly love these people if my physical health prevents me from engaging them at their point of need.

DAY 8

ELEVATE...with God's Word

And behold, a lawyer stood up to put him to the test, saying, "Teacher, what shall I do to inherit eternal life?" He said to him, "What is written in the Law? How do you read it?" And he answered, "You shall love the Lord your God with all your heart and with all your soul and with all your strength and with all your mind, and your neighbor as yourself." And he said to him, "You have answered correctly; do this, and you will live."

—Luke 10:25–28

For you were called to freedom, brothers. Only do not use your freedom as an opportunity for the flesh, but through love serve one another. For the whole law is fulfilled in one word: "You shall love your neighbor as yourself.

—Galatians 5:13–14

Husbands, love your wives, as Christ loved the church and gave himself up for her.

—Ephesians 5:25

EXCHANGE...with David Bush

Author Gary Chapman hit publishing paydirt years ago with his bestselling book *The Five Love Languages*.[1] The book reveals an all-too-common issue in marriages: We prefer to love our spouse the way we like to be loved or in a way that is more comfortable for us to express love rather than in a way that speaks love to them. Chapman asserts that if we can learn our mate's love language (how they prefer to receive love) and consistently speak it fluently through our words and actions, we will meet our biblical command *to live with them in an understanding way* and reap the benefits that come from a marriage that meets the needs of our spouse.

One of the basic responsibilities we're called to as followers of Christ is to love our neighbors as ourselves. It is my experience that obeying this command will mean asking myself, "What is my neighbor's 'love language?'" Demonstrating Jesus' love to my spouse, my children, my extended family, and my next-door neighbor will often involve the inconvenience of loving them in tangible ways that are naturally uncomfortable for me.

As I have sought to demonstrate love to other people and meet their needs, I've been struck how often these inconvenient opportunities involve physical labor.

- Sick, out-of-town, or widowed neighbors who need their lawns mowed or their driveways and sidewalks cleared of snow.

- Moving day for the single mom or family without the resources to have it done professionally.

- Leaf raking and gardening help for the couple whose husband is suffering from a debilitating disease.

- Walking or running in a fund-raiser for a cancer victim.

- The biannual church cleanup day.

- Cleaning the house for the family that is overwhelmed by foster care.

- The hospital visit that involves a one-mile round-trip journey by foot to the CCU from the remote parking garage.

Loving others as ourselves often involves a sacrifice of our time. Sometimes it comes at a financial cost. Loving another by being the first to apologize may cost us our pride. In addition to these, being Jesus to another will often necessitate a healthy physical body. Our willingness to even consider being involved in loving others—be they our spouse, our children, or our neighbors--will require clarity, awareness, vitality, and vigor. We will need a reserve of energy that can be drawn upon after meeting the needs of our employers, as well as our own personal needs. We will need the capacity to serve rather than be served.

Jesus is our perfect example of love in action. You can't read through the Gospel accounts of His life and ministry and not be confronted with the physical labor that was part of His daily experience. Remember the continuous travel by foot to reach villages with the gospel, the early mornings that stretched into late nights of healing and ministry, and the physical exertion it took to spend nights in prayer and do battle with demonic forces. The physiological ramifications of the passion and atonement on the cross alone are breathtaking.

Acknowledging that we don't have a picture of what His physical availability to love others into his latter years looks like, we can see from the trajectory of His life that Jesus was not going to let lifestyle choices get in the way of His capacity to love others. He spoke with authority when He called on us to love others like the Good Samaritan did in His famous parable. The Samaritan's loving response to the need of his neighbor was holistic, requiring a sacrifice of time, prejudice, finances, and physical strength. Bandaging, moving, and lifting a "dead weight" body onto his donkey came in addition to walking instead of riding to the next town.

In fulfilling the Great Commandment, are we remaining available to speak the love language of those needing our help? We were reminded years ago by a popular Christian band that "Luv is A Verb."[2] Indeed, loving our neighbor as ourselves is a command that demands our action.

EXPLORE...a Fresh Start

1. How, in your experience, has loving your neighbor necessitated a fit and healthy body?

2. In what ways do you like or need to be served that require fit and healthy people to meet your needs?

3. Have you experienced a connection between physical health and the capacity to serve others in spiritual work such as prayer and spiritual warfare?

4. What body care changes might need to happen that would allow you to love and serve others well into the future?

Notes:

ENJOY...a New You!

Enjoy the privilege of serving others out of your reservoir of energy and vitality! What joy there is in removing limitations on how we can be the hands and feet of Jesus!

Protecting my ability to love through physical service,

---

1. Gary Chapman. *The Five Love Languages: How To Express Heartfelt Commitment To Your Mate:* Chicago, IL Northfield Publishing, 1992.
2. DC Talk. "Luv Is A Verb," *Free At Last* (1992: Forefront Records; Brentwood, TN), CD.

My Ability To Fulfill The Great Commission Is Directly Impacted By The Health Of My Physical body.

ENGAGE...a New Day

My love for God and others will naturally flow out of my family and church to a broader impact on my community, my native country, and the world. My ability to engage Jesus' global directive will usually make physical demands on me that will necessitate a vital, healthy, and functioning physical body.

DAY 9

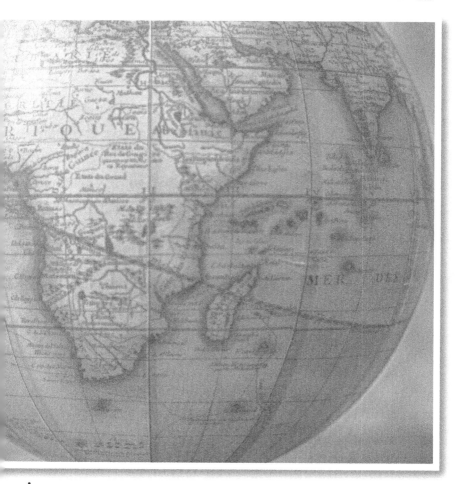

ELEVATE...with God's Word

And Jesus came and said to them, "All authority in heaven and on earth has been given to me. Go therefore and make disciples of all nations, baptizing them in the name of the Father and of the Son and of the Holy Spirit, teaching them to observe all that I have commanded you. And behold, I am with you always, to the end of the age.

—Matthew 28:18-20

Nevertheless, we have not made use of this right, but we endure anything rather than put an obstacle in the way of the gospel of Christ.

—1 Corinthians 9:12b

When I am with those who are weak, I share their weakness, for I want to bring the weak to Christ. Yes, I try to find common ground with everyone, doing everything I can to save some.

—1 Corinthians 9:22

EXCHANGE…with David Bush

At His ascension, Jesus gives a final, overarching command to His most intimate followers. The risen Son of God laid out His agenda to His disciples who had gathered on a hilltop in Galilee: Make disciples everywhere. Start in Jerusalem (where the Holy Spirit will empower you) and move out from there to Judea, Samaria, and the farthest reaches of known civilization. At the time, this command included many unknowns and details that would be revealed as the Spirit led His campaign to make the gospel known. But one thing would have been readily apparent: Jesus' strategy *involved a lot of walking.*

In our modern age of mass communication via websites, radio stations, cable and broadcast television, publications, and podcasts, it's easy to remove the physiological requirements Jesus' commission made on those receiving it. The disciples would be pursuing face-to-face gospel encounters over thousands of miles of civilized territory. Interestingly, we do not read in Acts that the physical demands that Jesus' commission made was a concern—or even a hindrance—to any of them. No one so much as demanded a donkey.

Fast-forward a couple thousand years, and some might

argue the Great Commission could be accomplished by pajama-clad basement dwellers possessing little more than a computer and a mouse. As easy as it would be to dismiss the need to be physically fit to be engaged in the Great Commission today, I would argue for deeper reflection regarding this assumption. I know of many who would not consider going on even a short-term mission trip because of the physical demands. I know of several who have been willing to go, but who have had to sit out for most of the practical work because of their physical inability to endure the work or conditions. Time changes, transcontinental airline flights, diet changes (both the quantity and quality of food), humidity changes, sleep changes, routine changes—all these call for a resiliency a growing number of Christians are unable to supply. It's no surprise that most mission trips today include recovery days in the midst of the work.

But the Great Commission includes more than trips to other countries. It means engaging with neighbors across town and across the street. This means we need the vitality and energy to develop relationships, meet needs, and provide practical assistance for our neighbors. When we're ready to eat dinner and settle in for a date with a good book or the television, the Great Commission will often ask us to be a redemptive influence in the lives of others. When God calls us to meet a need or share our faith, the right response is always "yes". He has promised to be with us in this supreme endeavor to the very end. Our responsibility is to remain available, prepared, and obedient.

Notes:

EXPLORE...a Fresh Start

1. God may ask you *to go to the ends of the earth.* Can you say *"yes"* to that call?

2. He will definitely provide opportunities to engage in gospel-centered ministry to people where you live. Are you physically ready to answer the call?

ENJOY...a New You!

This is your critical role! You've been intentionally chosen by God to be a part of His worldwide campaign of redemption!

Joining you on mission,

I Am Called By God To A Life Of Transformation.

ENGAGE…a New Day

Heaven is a wonderful benefit but not the goal and purpose for my calling as a child of God. My life purpose in Christ is to be marked by transformation from what I was before knowing Jesus, to a life that increasingly resembles Jesus. This transformation brings God glory.

ELEVATE...with God's Word

And we know that for those who love God all things work together for good, for those who are called according to his purpose. For those whom he foreknew he also predestined to be conformed to the image of his Son, in order that he might be the firstborn among many brothers.

—Romans 8:28–29

Do not be conformed to this world, but be transformed by the renewal of your mind, that by testing you may discern what is the will of God, what is good and acceptable and perfect.

—Romans 12:2

And we all, with unveiled face, beholding the glory of the Lord, are being transformed into the same image from one degree of glory to another. For this comes from the Lord who is the Spirit.

—2 Corinthians 3:18

As obedient children, do not be conformed to the passions of your former ignorance, but as he who called you is holy, you also be holy in all your conduct, since it is written, "You shall be holy, for I am holy."

—1 Peter 1:14-16

EXCHANGE…with David Bush

A good friend of mine related the story of the death of a close relative. "Aunt Betty" was a much-loved member of her local congregation. A deaconess and Sunday school teacher, Betty was quick to serve, quick to love, and always available to comfort those who needed to experience her generous embrace. It was a shock to all when a visitor to her home found her face down in front of her favorite rocker after experiencing a fatal heart attack at the age of 38. Her open Bible was found under her 300-pound frame.

At the funeral, grieving friends solemnly filed past Betty's oversized casket, and several were overheard remarking that "Betty was home now", that "she wouldn't come back if she could", and that "God loved her so much He took her home early." While well-meaning comments like these were intended to bring comfort to the family, my friend confessed that they felt misguided, if not outright untrue. Most were giving Betty a victory lap while my friend contemplated missed opportunities.

Stories like this reveal a basic misunderstanding in the church of God's goal and purpose for our lives. When surveyed, most Christians will answer the question, "What is God's goal for your life?" with the reply, "Heaven." While heaven is a wonderful benefit of knowing Christ as Savior, it is not God's goal for our lives as expressed in Scripture. God's goal for every believer is the same: transformation into the likeness of Christ. He will use Scripture and the Holy Spirit's work through our vocations, marriages, children, trials, illnesses, faithful friends, and victories to accomplish this work of transformation.

In the midst of a world system that is seeking to conform us to its values, priorities, and pursuits, God is glorified by demonstrating the power of the gospel to transform us from what we were before knowing Jesus, to those who increasingly reflect His values, priorities, and pursuits. A pursuit of holiness, made possible by the presence of the Holy Spirit, is God's goal for our lives, and it should be ours as well.

Most of us have seen this transformation at work in our own lives and in the lives of others. Formerly profane individuals who begin walking with Jesus find, through the power of the Holy Spirit and their cooperative obedience, their language changes over time. Those with toxic relationships see them begin to heal, materialists learn to submit their finances to the Lord, and worldly media choices transform to more godly offerings. This is a two steps forward and one step back affair for most, but tangible change does occur. It would raise concern if we saw no progress—or worse yet, movement in the wrong direction--from someone professing a sincere faith.

Each of us is a living testimony to the reality of that transformation. In as many years as God gives us and in as many ways as we are able, may we cooperate with God's goal of holistic transformation and glorify Him in the process.

Notes:

EXPLORE...a Fresh Start

1. Have you thought much about what God wants from your life?

2. Much emphasis is placed on the many things God gives us in Christ. Does it seem wrong somehow that God would have expectations of us as His children? If so, why?

3. What do you think brings God more glory: people hearing of your conviction that you're going to heaven after you die, or witnessing observable transformation in your life that makes you more like Jesus?

ENJOY...a New You!

Know that God has a daily purpose for you! Everything you experience—good, bad, difficult--can work toward His purpose of transformation.

Engaging in life transformation with you,

Dramatic Transformation In My Life Is Not Only Required, But Possible Because My Very Nature Has Been Changed.

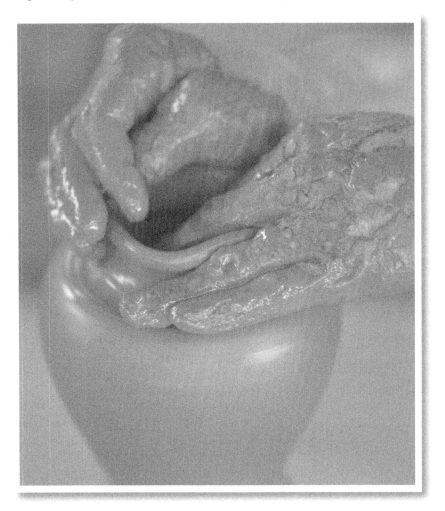

ENGAGE...a New Day

My salvation brought with it not just a clean record before God but a changed nature. The self-willed spirit I formerly possessed has been regenerated by the Holy Spirit, and His agenda is life-transformation.

DAY 11

ELEVATE...with God's Word

Therefore, if anyone is in Christ, he is a new creation. The old has passed away; behold, the new has come.

—2 Corinthians 5:17

I have been crucified with Christ. It is no longer I who live, but Christ who lives in me. And the life I now live in the flesh I live by faith in the Son of God, who loved me and gave himself for me.

—Galatians 2:20

We know that our old self was crucified with him in order that the body of sin might be brought to nothing, so that we would no longer be enslaved to sin. For one who has died has been set free from sin.

—Romans 6:6-7

His divine power has granted to us all things that pertain to life and godliness, through the knowledge of him who called us to his own glory and excellence, by which he has granted to us his precious and very great promises, so that through them you may become partakers of the divine nature, having escaped from the corruption that is in the world because of sinful desire.

—2 Peter 1:3–4

Do not lie to one another, seeing that you have put off the old self with its practices and have put on the new self, which is being renewed in knowledge after the image of its creator. Here there is not Greek and Jew, circumcised and uncircumcised, barbarian, Scythian, slave, free; but Christ is all, and in all.

—Colossians 3:9–11

EXCHANGE...with David Bush

Anyone who has engaged in a job search in recent years is aware there are numerous online companies interested in helping you through this gut-wrenching process. In addition to local and national job listings, these companies will customize your job search, upload your resume, and even let you know if your resume has been viewed by a prospective company. Another helpful feature is the company ratings provided by both current and former employees. Usually a one to five-star rating is given along with a paragraph as to why the rating was awarded.

I've encountered several of these sites, and it's interesting to note that nearly every intern gives the company a 5-star review. While it's possible interns are treated more deferentially than employees, my cynical side tells me there's more to it than that. Those who give lower scores are typically lower on the pecking order and closer to where the practical work gets done. Some of the standard comments accompanying these low scores are, "Cut back on help but expected the work to get done all the same." "I kept asking for the tools to do my job but was always told by management that because of cutbacks I'd have to make do." "So frustrating to want to do my best but foiled at every turn by incompetent management, bad information, and backstabbing."

If you've been to these sites, you know what I'm talking about. Perhaps you're commiserating with how close these comments resemble what you've said about your job! Interestingly, when it comes to the issue of life transformation, these same kinds of attitudes are often felt and expressed. We can look at the ambitious goal of life transformation God has for us and wonder how it's supposed to get done!

Left to our own devices, a transformation like this would be impossible; but God has given us all the tools necessary to accomplish His purposes in our lives. While I'll deal with the critical power that the presence of the Holy Spirit brings in another entry, it's necessary to understand that God can ask us to transform because He's given us a new nature. Our old nature—the part of us that would not cooperate with God in transformation—has been crucified (Romans 6:6–7) and replaced by a new nature that actually wants to cooperate with God's agenda. All who have been born again in Christ possess this new, cooperative nature. This is part of what makes us children of God instead of children of wrath (Ephesians 2:1–10).

It would be downright unfair for God to ask us to change things in our lives to which we've been naturally resistant, without providing the resources necessary to do the job. In fact, our sinful nature was so strong, Scripture tells us it would be *impossible* to make the changes God desires without His provision of an entirely different nature (Romans 8:7).

The changes God has in mind are not the "marginal" and "buff the edges" sort. Over time, and with our obedience, *massive* change is possible! The world, our flesh, and the Devil will provide headwinds, but our new nature in Christ is the game changer we all need to accomplish God's goal of life transformation. While I'd never think of my Heavenly

Father as an employer, I think we can all agree this kind of provision is worthy of a 5-star rating!

Notes:

EXPLORE...a Fresh Start

1. Have you ever felt like God expected more of you than you can deliver?

2. Finish this sentence: "Try as I might, I just never seem to be able to experience victory with _____."

3. What do today's Scripture and devotional have to say to that issue?

4. While our natures have been changed, we're still wrestling with the world, the flesh and the Devil. Which of these seems to provide the most consistent challenge to your transformation?

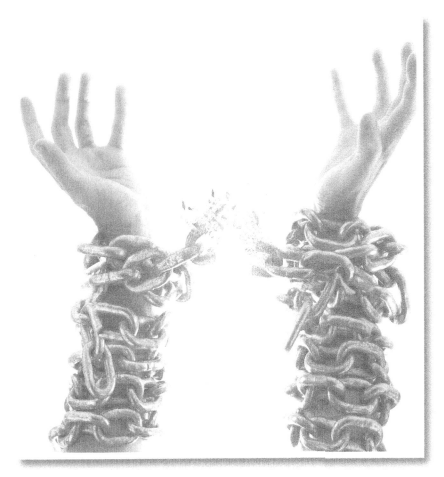

ENJOY...a New You!

Take joy in the reality that you actually want to please God. Before Christ changed you, you didn't.

Walking with you in the *new things that have come,*

God's Transformative Work In My Life Includes My Physical Body.

ENGAGE...a New Day

After redeeming my soul at the moment of salvation, God began a Spirit-empowered, holistic, and lifelong campaign of transformation. The gospel that redeemed my spirit is now the gospel that is at work redeeming my mind and body—and all the attitudes and actions that flow from them.

ELEVATE...with God's Word

Now may the God of peace himself sanctify you completely, and may your whole spirit and soul and body be kept blameless at the coming of our Lord Jesus Christ. He who calls you is faithful; he will surely do it.

—1 Thessalonians 5:23–24

But I discipline my body and keep it under control, lest after preaching to others I myself should be disqualified.

—1 Corinthians 9:27

I am speaking in human terms, because of your natural limitations. For just as you once presented your members as slaves to impurity and to lawlessness leading to more lawlessness, so now present your members as slaves to righteousness leading to sanctification.

—Romans 6:19

And I am sure of this, that he who began a good work in you will bring it to completion at the day of Jesus Christ.

—Philippians 1:6

EXCHANGE...with David Bush

An early heresy of the church was Gnosticism, which taught that the physical body was evil, and that a person could follow fleshly impulses without corrupting their spirit. The Bible teaches that our minds, bodies, and spirits are all intertwined, they influence each other, and all are the focus of the Holy Spirit's transformative campaign that moves us toward Christlikeness.

For believers, this transformation deals with renewing the thoughts, attitudes, preferences, biases, wounds, and prejudices we bring into our spiritual journey. Because so many of the changes the Spirit desires to work in our lives are spiritual, emotional, and intellectual, it would be easy to think that the "software" of our lives is the exclusive place where change is desired.

It's common in my interactions with people in need of physical transformation that I hear them quote 1 Timothy 4:8, "For while bodily training is of some value, godliness is of value in every way, as it holds promise for the present life and also for the life to come." This verse, which actually advocates for bodily training, is still seen as neutering the dozens of times Paul refers to exercising discipline and self-restraint in the physical sphere of our lives.

The notion that a Christ-follower can grow to full maturity while his body becomes a repository for chronic diseases is fiction. The Holy Spirit, Who will move us toward increasing generosity, greater love for others, a gentle spirit, and growing patience, is the same Spirit who is seeking to instill discipline and self-control that results in a functioning and available physical body.

People who struggle with body care are some of the nicest, kindest, generous, compassionate, competent people I know. In part, it is the current state of the Christian subculture that feeds the notion that someone can either develop their inner spiritual lives or care for the "superficial." But we can walk and chew gum at the same time. This "either-or" prospect is not scriptural.

Most Christians understand that growth in Christ means living counter-culturally. We will have to choose between using the language of the world, embracing the entertainment choices of the world, handling our money like the world—or pursuing Jesus.

Our approach to our bodies is no different. We must understand that the default of our culture is poor health. Follow the culture in your eating and exercise habits, and you will likely be overweight or obese, have high blood pressure, succumb to a chronic disease, and be on multiple prescriptions by the time you're in your 60s.

This is not transformation; it's capitulation.

"That won't happen to me," many tell themselves. "I played sports in high school and my grandfather lived to be 90 years old." Sadly, our declining national health statistics are made up of just such people. An unhealthy physical body has a tangible impact on both our minds and our spirits, and can have a deadening impact on both. This is one reason the Bible speaks about fasting as a way to clear our minds and our spirits so we can hear more clearly from God.

Our physical bodies will eventually break down and die, but that fact should not change our perspective of redemption. Death is the usurper, not the end envisioned by God at creation. We should be fighting death and decay, not advancing it or resigning ourselves to it. In Christ, we are given an ambitious example of conduct, temperament, faith, love, and sacrifice. He also foreshadows new, perfected bodies. In light of this, we seek His discipline and transformation in the physical realm as passionately as we seek it in the spiritual.

EXPLORE...a Fresh Start

1. When people talk about sanctification/transformation, do you reflexively think about character qualities and spiritual attributes?

2. The Apostle Paul often focuses on sexual conduct, not gluttony, when admonishing believers to bodily discipline. Why might this have been a bigger discipline issue in his day?

3. What do you see as some of the greatest challenges believers have today in the area of physical sanctification?

4. What are some steps you can take to pursue physical transformation?

ENJOY...a New You!

God's love and plan for you is so complete, He wants all of you—body, mind, and spirit!

Submitting to transformation with you,

Upon Conversion, My Body Plays Host To The Holy Spirit Of God.

ENGAGE...a New Day

God's Spirit, whose presence accompanied the Ark of the Covenant and filled the Holy of Holies in the tabernacle and the temple in the Old Testament, now seals and indwells believers in Christ. The preparation and reverence given these articles and places should be instructive to me as I consider the Spirit's home in my physical body today.

DAY 13

ELEVATE...with God's Word

Or do you not know that your body is a temple of the Holy Spirit within you, whom you have from God? You are not your own, for you were bought with a price. So glorify God in your body.

—1 Corinthians 6:19–20

And because you are sons, God has sent the Spirit of his Son into our hearts, crying, "Abba! Father!" So you are no longer a slave, but a son, and if a son, then an heir through God.

—Galatians 4:6-7

Do you not know that your bodies are members of Christ? Shall I then take the members of Christ and make them members of a prostitute? Never!

—1 Corinthians 6:15

With promises like this to pull us on, dear friends, let's make a clean break with everything that defiles or distracts us, both within and without. Let's make our entire lives fit and holy temples for the worship of God.

—2 Corinthians 7:1 (The Message)

EXCHANGE...with David Bush

Several years ago my wife, Beth, and I spent nearly two weeks on a study tour of Israel. One of the most stunning experiences of that memorable visit was the evening we went underground at the Temple Mount to view the original, massive foundation stones of Herod's Temple. Well below the current street level, these stones, along with the Western Wall (also part of the foundation) are all that remain of the original temple Herod built for the Jewish people beginning in 19 BC.

As we passed through dimly lit passageways along the base of the foundation, we suddenly came upon a small, cave-like nook that had been carved out of the foundation. It was only large enough to accommodate a few people, and was filled this particular evening with candles and two or three orthodox Jews who read fervent prayers from the

Torah. What would bring people hundreds of feet below the earth's surface to pray in obscurity in a carved-out niche in the temple's foundation?

Where we stood at that moment was, we were told, almost directly below the location of the former Holy of Holies—the inner chamber of the temple where the presence of the Holy Spirit dwelled between the cherubim that adorned the lid of the Ark of the Covenant. With Muslim control of the Temple Mount, and the Dome of the Rock that now stands there, this was as close as today's Jews would be able to get to the place that formerly hosted the very presence of God.

The temple and its most sacred space have always been held in the highest esteem possible by the people of Israel. David regretted that he lived in a palace while the old tabernacle of goat skins continued to host the presence of God. Nehemiah was furious to see the temple spaces get repurposed as condominiums for temple workers. Jesus twice cleaned out the court of the Gentiles when profit-minded marketers moved into an area reserved for prayer.

Read the instructions God gave for the construction of the articles that would fill the Temple and Holy of Holies, and you see the words *pure gold, silver, precious stones, fine, beautiful, elaborate, skilled,* and many other adjectives denoting quality and attention to detail. So awesome and sacred was the Holy of Holies that a specially selected and cleansed high priest could enter only once a year on the Day of Atonement to serve as an intercessor between the nation of Israel and their God.

By His death on the cross, Jesus made it possible for us

to experience the same kind of intimacy with God that only select priests had formerly enjoyed. This was illustrated by the tearing of the curtain that protected this space at the moment of Jesus' death on the cross. No longer constrained by the temple structure, the Holy Spirit now resides personally in the body of each person who repents and places their faith in Jesus for the forgiveness of their sins. Each of our bodies has become, as it were, individual "holy of holies" that carry with us the very presence of God.

Old Testament prophets and priests could hardly have conceived of our reality of permanently hosting the Spirit of God. While Old Testament passages hold glimmers of this possibility, such an unthinkable privilege would certainly require painstaking personal preparation and cleansing!

While it is God who must take the initiative and make us capable of receiving the indwelling presence of the Holy Spirit, the Apostle Paul makes clear the ramifications of His taking up residence within us: we are no longer owners, but have the responsibility of landlords. We take the Holy Spirit with us wherever we go, and we play host to His divine presence. What the orthodox Jewish prayer warriors were seeking via physical proximity to a former temple, is our daily experience when we know Christ personally!

EXPLORE...a Fresh Start

1. What connection do you see between the Holy Spirit's presence and body ownership as presented in the 1 Corinthians 6 passage above?

2. In the Old Testament, the Holy of Holies was off limits to all but the designated priest or high priest. According to the Galatians 4 passage above, what has changed God's accessibility to us with His personal indwelling?

   Do you think it's possible to become so familiar with this amazing truth that we miss the extent of the privilege we have as sons and daughters?

3. When you're going to host someone important in your home, what efforts do you make to clean up or set things in order? Is your attitude toward the Holy Spirit one of "He'll just have to put up with what I offer Him?"

ENJOY...a New You!

Recognizing the sanctifying work He is accomplishing in and through your body, God the Spirit is willing to reside there permanently while accomplishing His purposes through you!

A fellow transporter of the Holy Spirit's presence,

The Success Of My Transformation Is Based On Surrender To The Work Of The Holy Spirit.

ENGAGE...a New Day

My success in transforming toward Christlikeness will never be based on trying harder, but by surrendering more completely to the Holy Spirit's work in my life. I did not possess the ability to transform my spirit at the time of my salvation. Neither do I possess the capacity to align my mind or my body to Jesus' purposes through self-effort.

DAY 14

ELEVATE...with God's Word

How foolish can you be? After starting your new lives in the Spirit, why are you now trying to become perfect by your own human effort?

—Galatians 3:3 (NLT)

It is the Spirit who gives life; the flesh is no help at all. The words that I have spoken to you are spirit and life.

—John 6:63

But I say, walk by the Spirit, and you will not gratify the desires of the flesh. For the desires of the flesh are against the Spirit, and the desires of the Spirit are against the flesh, for these are opposed to each other, to keep you from doing the things you want to do.

—Galatians 5:16–17

EXCHANGE…with David Bush

Among the items I took with me when I left the business world for ministry nearly 20 years ago was a bent piece of stainless steel. I kept this custom-made tool as a reminder that my ideas of how people should do business are not nearly as important as helping them find success at what they know best.

I went to great lengths to try to re-engineer a system for ice cream dip store operators (which required my stainless steel adaptor) that had worked successfully for many years. While innovation certainly has its place, my attempts to "fix something that wasn't broken" were not successful and, in retrospect, not good business. I eventually enjoyed success when I ditched my system modifier and focused on working within the system already in place.

Our approach to the operating system of our lives in Christ can be just as frustrating. Our role in transformation is surrendering to the agent of change, the Holy Spirit, not trying harder to be good.

When we hear that the Holy Spirit is our *Helper* in the sanctification process, many of us envision a helpful and submissive co-pilot who might be called upon to take the wheel when we need to take a nap. With this picture of the

Holy Spirit's role, we are either underestimating the amount of work needed, or overestimating our ability to effect transformative change in our lives.

The Old Testament reveals that it is impossible to keep God's law perfectly. A frustrating and futile sacrificial system was put in place after the fall to deal with our inability to live holy lives under the Law.

Attempting to grow in Christlikeness today through self-effort is equally fruitless. For example, trying to get to a healthy lifestyle by making superficial changes like diets that can't be sustained, or limiting this food or that beverage won't work. It is like trying to keep the Law without a circumcised heart.

In the area of physical health and fitness, it is especially easy to believe we have an oversized ability to effect positive change as so much of our battle is behavioral. *I'll be more committed this time,* we tell ourselves. *I'll try harder and be more disciplined. I just need to stick with the program.*

The *program* we have been created in Christ to follow is surrender. This means consciously surrendering our total inability to pursue a balanced life to the Holy Spirit's complete ability to lead us to His desired result. When we have been making wrong health choices for a long time, we will need to become a different person inside to effect a long-term change.

Are you frustrated with fleshly innovations to spiritual growth that are not producing results? Perhaps it's time to surrender to the Holy Spirit's ability to achieve lasting transformation.

Notes:

EXPLORE...a Fresh Start

1. Do you agree with Jesus' statement that "the flesh is of no help at all" in the process of transformation? If so, what might you need to stop doing to see transformation take place? What is the only appropriate action we can engage in that will help this process move forward?

2. According to the Galatians 5 passage above, there is still a Spirit-empowered walk to engage in as well as Spirit-informed things to do. After surrendering your agenda and means of transformation, what actions might the Holy Spirit be prompting you to engage in that will move you toward holistic holiness?

3. What *better ideas* in bodily sanctification are you trying other than the biblical pattern of surrender and obedience?

ENJOY...a New You!

God's plan for your life transformation doesn't include the frustration or self-satisfaction that arises from doing things according to your fleshly impulses. He has a time-tested and proven pattern for success: surrender!

Waving the white flag with you,

Not Cooperating With The Holy Spirit's Goal Of Transforming My Mind And Body Causes Grief To Him And Hinders God's Work In My Life.

ENGAGE...a New Day

Grieving and quenching the Holy Spirit is not so much a matter of specific sins as much as it is a pattern of putting up barriers to the transformative work He desires to do in my life. I grieve the Spirit when I consistently resist the redemptive process moving me toward Christlikeness.

DAY 15

ELEVATE...with God's Word

And do not grieve the Holy Spirit of God, by whom you were sealed for the day of redemption.

—Ephesians 4:30

For those who live according to the flesh set their minds on the things of the flesh, but those who live according to the Spirit set their minds on the things of the Spirit. For to set the mind on the flesh is death, but to set the mind on the Spirit is life and peace. For the mind that is set on the flesh is hostile to God, for it does not submit to God's law; indeed, it cannot. Those who are in the flesh cannot please God.

—Romans 8:5–8

EXCHANGE…with David Bush

January 1, 1929, marks a day that will forever live in the annals of sports infamy. A New Year's Day crowd assembled for the 1929 Rose Bowl football game pitting The University of California, Berkeley Golden Bears against the Georgia Tech Yellow Jackets. Football fans would witness one of the most bizarre blunders in football history.

The capacity crowd, most of whom were Cal Berkley fans, were hopeful the Bears could prevent Georgia Tech from winning a second consecutive National Championship. A standout for the Berkley Bears was Roy Riegel, an All-Coast Team member and future All-American who played both offense and defense.

Riegel's opportunity for lasting glory came late in the second quarter, when he recovered a fumble by Georgia Tech's Jack "Stumpy" Thomason just 30 yards from the Yellow Jackets' goal line. Rather than streaking into the end zone for the score, Riegel got turned around in the post-fumble skirmish and ended up racing 69 yards towards his own goal line. Players and fans alike screamed for Riegel to turn around, but in the cacophony, he was unaware of his misdirected enthusiasm. One of his own teammates finally caught up with him on the one-yard line and prevented him from scoring for the opponents.

Rather than trying to run their offense so close to their goal line, Cal elected to punt from inside their own end zone. The punt was blocked, and the resulting 2-point safety became the deciding factor in Cal's 8-7 loss. Ever since that day, "Wrong Way Roy Riegel" has become a lasting metaphor for counterproductive behavior.

Fortunately, "Wrong Way Roy's" most famous accomplishment didn't define him personally. He went on to accomplish much, both as a football player and a citizen. But the high profile of his improbable dash has made it a part of football lore.[1]

When it comes to our personal sanctification, we often follow in the footsteps of "Wrong Way Roy." Both unintentionally and willfully we find ourselves working at cross purposes with the Holy Spirit's goal for our lives, which is transformation to the likeness of Christ. The Spirit's agenda is focused on redeeming us from the kinds of attitudes and actions that typified our behavior prior to knowing Jesus. His agenda moves us from a profane tongue to one that edifies and blesses, and from a materialistic mindset to one of generosity. The Spirit takes relationships that were broken and makes them whole again. Whether it involves our thoughts or our actions, His agenda is progressive redemption. This process will continue throughout our lifespan, and it foreshadows an ultimate day of redemption when His work will be complete, including a new, imperishable body.

When we continuously erect barriers to His redemptive

work, we grieve Him. Think of this not so much as isolated, specific sins that bring momentary grief, but as a lifestyle pattern we refuse to surrender to the Spirit's transformative work.

The Holy Spirit is moving us toward the goal line of sanctification but, because of our ignorance, confusion, or willfulness, we're heading in the opposite direction–perhaps even turning a deaf ear to those imploring us to turn around.

We all grieve the Spirit in many ways through our lack of cooperation. It is my belief that in the church, a common barrier is a lack of bodily discipline. While the Spirit seeks to lead us toward habits and behaviors that will increase our functionality, vitality, and availability, many persist in pursuing unhealthy behaviors. People are seemingly unconcerned about the inertia this creates in their transformative progress.

How can we get on the same page as the Holy Spirit? We stop running. We listen to what God's Word and godly people counsel for our lives. We repent, turn around, and surrender to the power of the Spirit to make consistent progress in the right direction. That is a winning game plan!

EXPLORE...a Fresh Start

Notes:

1. Have you thought much about God's big picture agenda of life transformation? Have you thought about how you can either be cooperating with that agenda or putting up barriers?

2. How might you encourage others you see running the wrong way in some area of sanctification?

3. What attitudes and actions might identify you as a "Wrong Way Roy" in the arena of life transformation?

4. What would it look like to repent and head toward the goal of redemption?

ENJOY...a New You!

The Holy Spirit never gives up on us, but remains to coach, encourage, and bring us victory!

Journeying with you toward the goal,

---

1. Wikipedia.2019. "Roy Riegels," https://en.wikipedia.org/wiki/Roy_Riegels, June 21, 2019.

God Is Not Waiting Until I Achieve An Ultimate Goal To Take Pleasure In My Journey.

ENGAGE...a New Day

God is celebrating every step of obedience taken in faith. He is not standing at some arbitrary finish line to give His commendation. I can and should sense His pleasure and assistance throughout my journey of body stewardship.

ELEVATE...with God's Word

The Lord directs the steps of the godly. He delights in every detail of their lives.

—Psalm 37:23 (NLT)

Therefore, my beloved, as you have always obeyed, so now, not only as in my presence but much more in my absence, work out your own salvation with fear and trembling, for it is God who works in you, both to will and to work for his good pleasure.

—Philippians 2:12–13

And Jesus increased in wisdom and in stature and in favor with God and man.

—Luke 2:52

Therefore, since we are surrounded by so great a cloud of witnesses, let us also lay aside every weight, and sin which clings so closely, and let us run with endurance the race that is set before us, looking to Jesus, the founder and perfecter of our faith, who for the joy that was set before him endured the cross, despising the shame, and is seated at the right hand of the throne of God.

—Hebrews 12:1–2

EXCHANGE…with David Bush

Their stories are well documented now; former contestants of the hit show *The Biggest Loser* returning to their former lifestyles—and the resultant morbid obesity—once the cameras, the national fame, and the ever-present encouragement from their coaches came to an end.

A local version of this storyline came to my attention recently. Scrolling through social media, I noticed photos and postings from someone who a couple of years previously had achieved notoriety for his massive weight loss. His well-publicized journey out of morbid obesity had garnered social media buzz, public speaking invitations, and even a well-produced promotional video from a national fitness center he frequented.

Now his timeline featured photos reminiscent of the before

pictures he used to post, along with links and recipes for indulgent desserts and references to what fast foods he was craving. What happened?

It's possible that the accolades and positive reinforcement he was receiving throughout his long slog to better health was the lifeline that kept him moving forward toward a healthy weight. Accolades like "You look awesome!!"…"Way to go, bro!!"…"You are such an inspiration!!" were the daily soundtrack of his life during that season.

Upon arriving at his goal, however, he experienced what others in his situation do: The *new normal* is expected. No one is cheering health maintenance with the same fervor as the dramatic pursuit.

So it is with the *all or nothing* trap that ensnares us all in the arena of sanctification. If we're not *all in* at any given moment, we find it easy to let past disobedience become the template for our lives, until we have more momentum in the right direction.

This way of thinking is fostered by the picture of Jesus standing at some arbitrary finish line, waiting for us to arrive before He can affirm our progress. If we can't finish, the thinking goes, we might as well give up. It should encourage us to know that while God exists outside our space and time limitations, He is also a God who works through process in our reality of time. He created the world and its living beings progressively in six days. Jesus matured physiologically like any normal child. Both of these examples were considered *good* and *pleasing* to God.

We need to remember there are more than a great cloud of witnesses cheering our own progress in faith and stewardship. Jesus is there too, rejoicing in every step of obedience. He's not standing at the finish line. He's walking with us.

Notes:

EXPLORE…a Fresh Start

1. What can we learn from creation regarding God being a God of process…and enjoying that process and seeing it as good?

2. What would we miss in our life experiences if we were able to leap forward to success and completion without the trials, failures, successes, and wisdom that is gained along the way? How helpful would you be to others in a transformative journey if everything happened easily and quickly for you?

3. How might our two steps forward and one step back journey of transformation this side of eternity provoke greater praise and worship in the new heaven and earth?

ENJOY...a New You!

God is patient with you and enjoying the process He's designed, and is working in you for His good pleasure.

Joyful in today's progress (while keeping an eye on the prize!),

Dave

A Fit And Available Body Is The Fruit Of A Life That Is Exercising Self-Control, A Natural Outcome Of A Life Led By The Spirit.

ENGAGE...a New Day

A life surrendered to the control of the Holy Spirit exhibits the characteristics of the Spirit. Among these Christ-like qualities are discipline and self-control, which are demonstrated in my temperament, the handling of my finances, and my body care.

Day 17

ELEVATE...with God's Word

But I say, walk by the Spirit, and you will not gratify the desires of the flesh.
—Galatians 5:16

But the fruit of the Spirit is love, joy, peace, patience, kindness, goodness, faithfulness, gentleness, self-control; against such things there is no law.
—Galatians 5:22–23

For this very reason, make every effort to supplement your faith with virtue, and virtue with knowledge, and knowledge with self-control, and self-control with steadfastness, and steadfastness with godliness, and godliness with brotherly affection, and brotherly affection with love. For if these qualities are yours and are increasing, they keep you from being ineffective or unfruitful in the knowledge of our Lord Jesus Christ. For whoever lacks these qualities is so nearsighted that he is blind, having forgotten that he was cleansed from his former sins. Therefore, brothers, be all the more diligent to confirm your calling and election, for if you practice these qualities you will never fall.

—2 Peter 1:5–10

EXCHANGE...with David Bush

Discipline and self-control have never been easy. Highlighting this fact is the fourteenth century true story of Duke Raynald III, a man whose lack of discipline literally imprisoned him. Raynald, who was nicknamed *Crassus*, meaning *fat,* lived in what is now Belgium. Grossly overweight, he was imprisoned in a room with no locks or doors after a succession dispute with his younger brother Edward. Edward promised Raynald he could regain his title and property whenever he was able to leave the room.

For the average person this would not have been a challenge, as the doorway and window exits were of normal size. But Raynald's morbidity was so great, it would have required uncharacteristic restraint to lose the weight necessary to gain his freedom.

Knowing his brother's lack of self-control, Edward delivered delicacies to Raynald each day, ensuring his size would continue to imprison him. When accused by his detractors of cruelty, Edward had a ready answer: "My brother is not a prisoner. He may leave when he so wills."

Raynald's lack of discipline left him imprisoned in the room for ten years. After Edward's death in battle, he was released. However, due to poor health, he ruled in his brother's place for less than a year.

Perhaps the most challenging of the Spirit's qualities to display are discipline and self-control. These attributes involve delayed gratification, self-denial, and even deprivation and pain. While many see the benefit for athletes-in-training or those in the military, their relevance to the Christian life has faded in recent generations. When was the last time you were invited to attend a conference focusing on the spiritual disciplines of prayer, fasting, solitude, journaling, and Scripture memorization? I know from personal experience that generating excitement for a body stewardship conference can be a tough sell!

Achieving consistent discipline and self-control by our own effort is an impossible task. Left to our own devices, we can only attempt change by *gutting it out* or *trying harder.* Thankfully, the Spirit is aware of our inability to enact lasting change. Instead of asking us to reach deeper into a supply of self-control that doesn't exist, He implores us to surrender more deeply to His limitless supply.

It is critical to remember we are trying to imitate the Spirit, not create a better version of ourselves. Accomplishing this means asking for His help and then allowing Him to take control. Requesting help and then going back to the same self-effort that has proved fruitless in the past is the biblical definition of foolishness (Gal. 3:3).

Are you in bondage because of a lack of discipline and self-control? The world will continue to provide daily opportunities to remain imprisoned. The solution to your dilemma is not to *try harder* or *reach deeper* but to surrender more completely.

Surrender to what?

Surrender to your complete inability and God's limitless ability. Surrender your logical or worldly thinking to the Spirit's supernatural and grace-saturated approach. Surrender your narcissistic tendencies to Jesus' others-centered strategy. Surrender your need to earn God's approval to an acceptance that God loves you in spite of you.

Surrendering to the Spirit's control is a continual choice that involves dying to ourselves so we can remain available for God's purposes. This daily death allows the cross of Christ to grow larger in our lives as we recognize our inability to transform ourselves. In this way, the gospel becomes a daily reality for us as we pursue the holiness of Jesus.

Like the fourteenth century glutton Duke Raynold, III, we each have a daily decision to make that will either lead us toward a goal of self-control or leave us imprisoned by undisciplined lives.

Notes:

EXPLORE...a Fresh Start

1. Where do you struggle in the area of discipline and self-control?

2. Have you experienced the frustration of *trying harder* without lasting results? What is the difference between *living the Christian life* and Christ living His life through you?

3. What needs to be surrendered to the control of the Holy Spirit that would bring needed discipline to your life?

☑ Love
☑ Joy
☑ Peace
☑ Patience
☑ Kindness
☑ Goodness
☑ Faith
☑ Gentleness
☑ Self-contr

ENJOY...a New You!

Jesus' yoke is easy and His burden is light when we enlist the assistance of His Helper, the Holy Spirit, to do the heavy lifting!

Trying to remember to stay yoked to Jesus,

My Motive For Pursuing A Fit Life Is More Important To God Than My Intentions Or My Results.

My goals for this year:

ENGAGE...a New Day

God is primarily concerned with my motives and heart attitudes, even when they involve the pursuit of behaviors He views as commendable and appropriate. Just as with giving and moral living, there are wrong motives for pursuing a physically fit life.

DAY 18

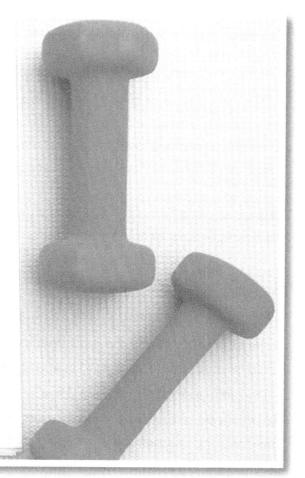

ELEVATE...with God's Word

People may be pure in their own eyes, but the LORD examines their motives.

—Proverbs 16:2 (NLT)

For the LORD sees not as man sees: man looks on the outward appearance, but the LORD looks on the heart.

—1 Samuel 16:7b

To the weak I became weak, that I might win the weak. I have become all things to all people, that by all means I might save some. I do it all for the sake of the gospel, that I may share with them in its blessings.

—1 Corinthians 9:22–23

For I am not aware of anything against myself, but I am not thereby acquitted. It is the Lord who judges me. Therefore do not pronounce judgment before the time, before the Lord comes, who will bring to light the things now hidden in darkness and will disclose the purposes of the heart. Then each one will receive his commendation from God.

—1 Corinthians 4:4–5

Each one must give as he has decided in his heart, not reluctantly or under compulsion, for God loves a cheerful giver.

—2 Corinthians 9:7

You ask and do not receive, because you ask wrongly, to spend it on your passions.

—James 4:3

EXCHANGE...with David Bush

My second year of college I was elected vice president of the student body. In this role, I was to organize campus activities that would be student-led, be broad in appeal, and foster education and the arts. Upon hearing I was a singer, songwriter, and performer with musical connections to professional musicians (including one enrolled at the college), our faculty advisor and other student government leaders enthusiastically endorsed my presenting a concert in the well-appointed campus performing arts center.

With a generous budget, and contacts in media and promotion, a great opportunity presented itself for a student-led event that would showcase my music to a new audience. In what seemed like a work of Providence, I was enrolled at the time in a stage lighting and production class. I suggested the class use my concert as a real-world opportunity to develop and execute a public event I hoped would be of far more interest to them than what our planned curriculum would offer. They enthusiastically agreed.

While most of my music at the time was secular in content, I had a couple of Christian-themed songs in my repertoire. How cool would it be, I thought, if I performed one of them to a largely unbelieving audience? The positive impact this might have on the spiritually lost seemed like the cherry on top of a wonderful opportunity.

The concert promotional campaign was ambitious. Posters of me were all over the campus. A professional photographer had developed a storyboard concept to introduce me to the public that included a blonde model more interested in my chest hair than my music. While I had misgivings about the approach, I went along with it because the photographer— the expert in these matter—was very insistent. I tried to convince myself that it was a marketing necessity to be presented as desirable by beautiful women.

The concert itself was quite the spectacle, with big sound and lots of lighting effects and smoke (thanks to my classmates). A photographer I hired captured all of it for posterity. The concert closed with me giving a brief testimony of my faith and playing a song I hoped would connect with the lost in the audience.

A couple of days after the concert, I stopped by the office of the stage and lighting design professor to collect what I assumed would be a "thanks for letting us be a part of this great event" payday.

I received a very different response than I expected. "Your classmates busted their butts for you," he stated tersely. "There was no sense of gratitude expressed…it seemed to be all about you. Frankly, everyone pretty much felt used."

I could not have been more sobered. It was as though the prophet Nathan had pointed his finger at me and stated, "You are the man!" I remember leaving the office, stepping behind a brick pillar in the courtyard, and weeping. My professor's words brought clarity and conviction to the motives that had been driving me from the onset. As hard as it was to admit, the whole affair had been about me, my image, my notoriety, my success. My *intentions,* and those of others, to produce a campus event that showcased the abilities and contributions of students, never reached its potential because the attention was solely focused on me. Those attending undoubtedly enjoyed the finished product, the result of all the efforts. But those involved in the process of producing those results felt used and disrespected.

With the clarity that the Holy Spirit's conviction brought, I tearfully considered what kind of dysfunctional testimony I had provided through my words, music, promotional campaign and self-serving actions.

God has always cared about motives more than intentions or results. The scriptural biographies of Saul and David make this abundantly clear. But this is true in all of life, including our pursuit of physical transformation. Our motives will be driving the process long after the inaction of our intentions has faded away. The result of better health will not ultimately be God-glorifying if the process used to arrive at that destination was not stirred by a gospel-inspired motive.

When our intentions become nothing more than wishful thinking and sins of omission, heart motives move us to action. When we're focused on results, we need to remember that God is focused on process. If you're in search of a motive that is biblically sound and gospel-centered, may I suggest one? The guiding statement of Fit For The King, the body stewardship ministry I lead, defines our motive in terms of *physical availability*:

Being Fit For The King means being physically available to love God completely, let Him love others through you, and accomplish all He desires with you for His glory.[1]

EXPLORE...a Fresh Start

1. What intentions have you had in the area of body care? Have they led to consistent action?

2. What results do you desire to see in your level of health and fitness? What does God get out of those results?

3. What was the Apostle Paul's motive for maximizing his availability to share truth with others in 1 Corinthians 9:22–23?

4. Have you arrived at a gospel-centered motive for changing unhealthy behaviors or maintaining sound behaviors? Are you being honest with yourself and God about your motives?

ENJOY...a New You!

God loves you so intimately, He's even concerned with the motives behind your efforts toward godliness.

Trying to keep my motives pure,

1. David Bush, *Fit For The King: Your Health And God's Purpose For Your Life.* (Des Moines, Iowa: King of Kings Publishing 2015), page 29.

Satan Does Not Care What I Obsess Over As Long As It Isn't Jesus.

ENGAGE...a New Day

If Satan can't imprison me in a life of physical neglect and unavailability, he's just as happy to push me through a healthy pursuit of physical availability to obsession with fitness. The great deceiver doesn't care what I'm worshiping as long as it isn't Jesus.

Day 19

ELEVATE...with God's Word

The thief comes only to steal and kill and destroy. I came that they may have life and have it abundantly

—John 10:10

Put on the whole armor of God, that you may be able to stand against the schemes of the devil.

—Ephesians 6:11

For where your treasure is, there your heart will be also.

—Matthew 6:21

Do not love the world or the things in the world. If anyone loves the world, the love of the Father is not in him. For all that is in the world—the desires of the flesh and the desires of the eyes and pride of life—is not from the Father but is from the world.

—1 John 2:15–16

But I am afraid that, as the serpent deceived Eve by his craftiness, your minds will be led astray from the simplicity and purity of devotion to Christ.

—2 Corinthians 11:3

EXCHANGE...with David Bush

Satan knows better than anyone that created beings were made to worship their Creator. As Lucifer, he was the worship leader of the heavenly host that surrounded the throne of God. Corrupted by pride, he was dispatched from heaven and has been on a campaign ever since to promote false objects of worship to those who bear God's image.

Satan is a master deceiver, continuously providing unworthy objects or goals as the focus of our lives. He knows we need to worship something, and he works with our cooperative flesh to erect a fresh supply of idols. Many of these pursuits are laudible, but they keep us self-satisfied so that we never seriously consider our need for a Savior or give Him the worship He deserves.

Christians are not immune to worshiping idols of the heart. We often pursue good and beneficial endeavors with a fervor that Jesus alone deserves. In my experience, physiological goals are a common idol. I have often seen unfit people pursue beneficial physical change in their lives with a passion I have never observed in their pursuit of other spiritual disciplines. Their progress is often catalogued with *before* and *after* photos depicting dramatic physical change. I can't help but wonder if there has been any spiritual transformation toward Christlikeness.

That which captivates our hearts and our minds is what we worship. In the midst of a culture that offers every imaginable distraction, it takes tenacious discipline to keep our eyes on the prize of following after Jesus. Whether it's political or financial turmoil, a news cycle that feeds on crisis, a relationship or health goal we're pursuing, or a career we're building, there is no shortage of suitors for our hearts.

It is because of this tendency to obsess that I am not a big fan of commercial diet plans. In addition to not being sustainable, most diet programs tend to move the participant into an all-encompassing pursuit of compliance. "*Never* eat this." "*Always* eat this." "Always eat *this* with *this*." "Never eat *this* food group." "*Only* eat this food group." Measure, weigh, calculate, tabulate. In the end, a *diet* gets the credit for improved health, not God's work of self-discipline in our lives.

Those pursuing a high level of fitness can become laser-focused on their goals. I've known many people who would never miss a workout but for whom church or Bible study attendance is optional. Bodybuilders are especially susceptible in this area. Eating just the right foods and supplementing with just the right products at just the right time is a daily routine for those serious about this pursuit. I know one young lady so captivated by her goal to compete as a bodybuilder that her relationships with family, co-workers and friends at church died on the altar of her eating and workout schedule.

As is true with any earthly pursuit not inspired by the Holy Spirit, those who give themselves to a physiological or athletic goal rarely feel they have *arrived.* The elusive nature of these kinds of goals leads many to employ means of achieving them that end up robbing them of their long-term health. While it is true that most Christians would benefit from increased attention to their nutrition and exercise regimens, Satan is happy to push a believer through a balanced, sustainable lifestyle into obsession with all things fitness.

If only Jesus received this kind of devotion, discipline, and focus!

When we allow the gospel to guide our body care, we know our priorities will remain healthy and balanced. With Jesus as our center, our motives will be tempered by the security of His love and the superiority of His rule. He is not a tyrant who demands slavish submission or an ambitious coach who despises weakness and imperfection. Jesus is the loving leader who alone is worthy of our obsession and worship.

EXPLORE...a Fresh Start

1. Think for a minute about your thought life; where do your thoughts tend to go, what do you daydream about, fantasize about, and plan for? Is there a common thread?

2. Does Scripture indicate Jesus had to expend much thought or energy on His diet or exercise regimen? What are some practical reasons why this did not consume much of His attention? If you moved with intentionality, remained active, and ate to fuel yourself (versus pleasure, boredom, stress, and entertainment), would you need to obsess over any aspect of your physical life?

3. What is the ratio of time you spend each week on fitness-related pursuits versus prayer, study of God's Word, worship and service to others?

ENJOY...a New You!

Obsession with Jesus sets us free from an excessive and un-balanced pursuit of fitness. He is enough. He satisfies.

Trying to keep Jesus at the center of everything,

It Is Entirely Possible To Be Physically Fit And Spiritually Lost.

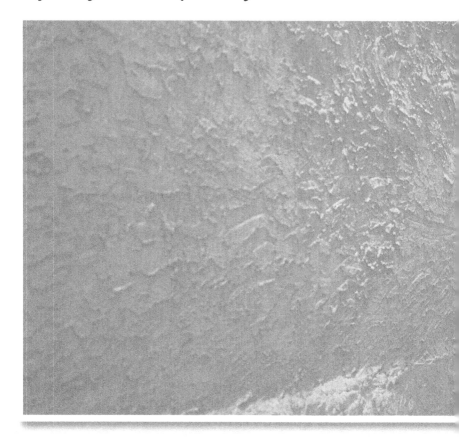

ENGAGE...a New Day

While my body received a death sentence at the fall through Adam, my spirit is still eternal. It is this eternal part of my being that is God's initial focus in the redemption story. Buffing and polishing the veneer while the core of my being rots may impress those drawn to the superficial, but God is not impressed. He can have no fellowship with an unredeemed façade.

DAY 20

ELEVATE...with God's Word

When they came, he looked on Eliab and thought, "Surely the Lord's anointed is before him." But the Lord said to Samuel, "Do not look on his appearance or on the height of his stature, because I have rejected him. For the Lord sees not as man sees: man looks on the outward appearance, but the Lord looks on the heart."

—1 Samuel 16:6–7

"Woe to you, scribes and Pharisees, hypocrites! For you are like white-washed tombs, which outwardly appear beautiful, but within are full of dead people's bones and all uncleanness.

—Matthew 23:27

Do not let your adorning be external—the braiding of hair and the putting on of gold jewelry, or the clothing you wear…

—1 Peter 3:3

EXCHANGE…with David Bush

Jesus' teaching about the Kingdom of God in the Beatitudes begins with the foundational issue of our lost state of being. "Blessed are the poor in spirit,"He begins. Before we can enter the Kingdom, we must realize our spiritual poverty and our great need. Later, in His encounter with the rich young ruler, Jesus laments, "It is hard for the rich to inherit the Kingdom of God." (Matthew 19:23) People's wealth, beauty, and intellect serve to insulate them from a recognition of their spiritual poverty.

A healthy and fit physical body can also numb us to the reality of our spiritual brokenness.

People see and may be impressed with our physical appearance, and assume the well-nourished body houses a soul that is equally healthy. But our souls need to be more than *healthy*. They need to be perfect, pure, and holy. Only Jesus' forgiveness and presence can accomplish that.

On our own, we can pursue physical health and actually achieve it for a time. But none of us is naturally pursuing a right relationship with God; this is something He initiates and perfects. Building a strong and resilient body can become a barrier to a relationship with God, as it has the potential to fill us with pride and self-sufficiency.

This was true in the life of a good friend of mine who spent years chiseling his body to perfection. While this pursuit was born out of a hunger for acceptance, identity, and a deep lack of self-worth, it also served to insulate him from addressing the emptiness of his spiritual life. *Everyone thinks I've got it all together,* he thought before his conversion, *and who am I to tell them they're wrong?*

I've met a lot of people like my friend. They have financial security. They have their health. Their level of fitness earns them compliments and respect from others. And they're not about to expose the secret most who are successful share: It's still not enough, and it doesn't fill the aching void in their lives only Jesus can satisfy. Healthy people have the same sin problem as everyone else, and the gospel alone has the power to set free all who are captive to sin, including the physically fit.

Notes:

EXPLORE...a Fresh Start

1. Imagine personally meeting Jesus in the course of your day. Do you hope he would be impressed by your physique? Have you ever thought to yourself, "God is sure lucky someone like me acknowledges Him and gives Him some street cred"?

2. Do you see yourself as being lost, helpless, and hopeless without Jesus' saving grace in your life?

3. Do you view your good health (if you have it) more as a result of something you've earned or as a gift from God?

Visit *https:///www.storiesfromthewell.org* to view transformational testimonies from those whose lives have been changed through a relationship with Jesus Christ and to gain a clear understanding of the gospel.

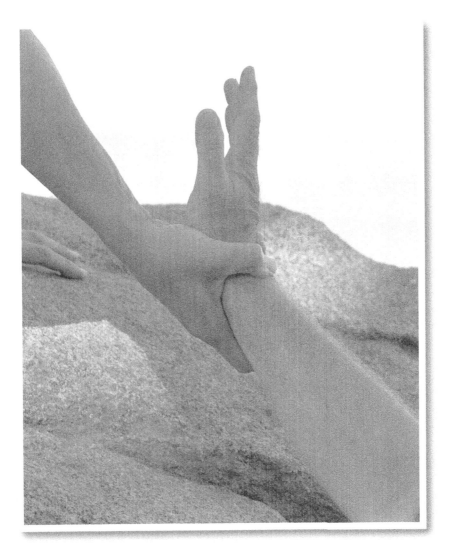

ENJOY...a New You!

God can see through all of our veneers to what really matters to Him—our hearts.

Praying you experience good health and appropriate spiritual poverty in equal measure,

My Status As A Saved And Sealed Believer Does Not Make Me Immune To The God-Ordained Principles Of Sowing, Reaping, And Compound Return That Govern Life, Including My Physical Health.

ENGAGE...a New Day

As a Christian, I experience the same consequences and blessings for foolish and wise behavior as I did before I knew the Lord. While I am free from the ultimate judgment and condemnation for foolishness others outside of Christ will receive, God does not override the cause and effect of my behaviors and decisions simply because I am saved.

DAY 21

ELEVATE...with God's Word

Do not be deceived: God is not mocked, for whatever one sows, that will he also reap. For the one who sows to his own flesh will from the flesh reap corruption, but the one who sows to the Spirit will from the Spirit reap eternal life.

—Galatians 6:7–8

Everyone who comes to me and hears my words and does them, I will show you what he is like: he is like a man building a house, who dug deep and laid the foundation on the rock. And when a flood arose, the stream broke against that house and could not shake it, because it had been well built. But the one who hears and does not do them is like a man who built a house on the ground without a foundation. When the stream broke against it, immediately it fell, and the ruin of that house was great.

—Luke 6:47–49

My experience shows that those who plant trouble and cultivate evil will harvest the same.

—Job 4:8 (NLT)

David said to Nathan, "I have sinned against the Lord." And Nathan said to David, "The Lord also has put away your sin; you shall not die. Nevertheless, because by this deed you have utterly scorned the Lord, the child who is born to you shall die."

—2 Samuel 12:13–14

And Moses lifted up his hand and struck the rock with his staff twice, and water came out abundantly, and the congregation drank, and their livestock. And the Lord said to Moses and Aaron, "Because you did not believe in me, to uphold me as holy in the eyes of the people of Israel, therefore you shall not bring this assembly into the land that I have given them."

—Numbers 20:11–12

Whoever sows injustice will reap calamity, and the rod of his fury will fail.

—Proverbs 22:8

For they sow the wind, and they shall reap the whirlwind.

—Hosea 8:7a

Let us not become weary in doing good, for at the proper time we will reap a harvest if we do not give up.

—Galatians 6:19

EXCHANGE...with David Bush

I moved from my native Southern California to Iowa over 30 years ago, trading beaches and traffic for farm fields and a better commute. Des Moines, the city in which I reside, has all the amenities of most large metropolitan areas and hosts one of the largest financial and insurance centers in the world. Drive just a few miles outside the metro area, however, and all you can see in the spring and summer are rolling hills awash in green.

Agriculture and finance are daily topics of conversation in these parts, something we share with both Jesus and the Apostle Paul. Sowing, reaping, and compound return are principles that are on display throughout the Old Testament, the Gospels and the Epistles. These are principles that govern the life of the Christian as well as the unbeliever, with both positive and negative implications.

Joseph and his brothers in the Old Testament are early examples of this principle. Sold into slavery by his jealous brothers, Joseph faithfully honored God with his life through extraordinary hardship and disappointment in Egypt over many years. He reaped an abundant harvest of compound return in the space of a day when he was elevated to second-in-command of Egypt by Pharaoh. Upon traveling to Egypt to buy grain, his brothers found their years of plotting and deception reaped a sudden and bitter harvest of hardship and turmoil.

In the days of the judges, Eli the Priest and his sons Hophni and Phineas were doing some sowing and reaping of their own. Eli's sons conspired to profane the Lord's sacrificial system and fornicated with the women serving at the temple gates while Eli turned a blind eye. After years of bad behavior and warnings from God, all three suddenly died on the same day.

David the shepherd boy faithfully walked with God in obscurity even after being anointed as Israel's future king. An unscheduled and unthinkable battlefield appointment with the Philistine giant Goliath transformed him into a national hero in one afternoon.

Jesus illustrates these principles with a parable about two men who build two different kinds of houses. One is built slowly on a firm foundation. Another is erected on sand, without the time and expense of laying a solid foundation. One stands in the storm; the other is suddenly and catastrophically destroyed.

Sowing, reaping, and compound return. I know many who comprehend and apply these principles as they relate to relationships, finances, educational pursuits and their jobs. Many of these same people seem unaware that these principles are at work in our physical bodies as well.

As a pastor who has spent many years doing hospital visitation, I can attest to the fact that years of poor food choices and physical inactivity will eventually result in a health crisis "nobody saw coming." My experience is that while God is often merciful and gracious in sparing lives, Christians and non-Christians reap similar consequences from the seed they sow. Responding to the unbiblical notion that we can avoid the consequences of our behavior, the Apostle Paul states, "Do not be deceived, God is not mocked."

Sowing, reaping, and compound return are biblical principles, not guarantees. Whether or not we experience the compound return of a great harvest in the here and now, we can be assured

God sees the diligence and perseverance with which we are investing in our long-term availability for the sake of the Kingdom.

My testimony is that sowing good fitness habits has allowed me to reap a bountiful harvest of experiences with my family and kept me fully engaged in productive ministry. By God's continuing mercies, I hope the seed I sow today will provide a wonderful harvest of active experiences with my grandchildren and fruitful ministry long into the future.

EXPLORE...a Fresh Start

1. How have you seen the principle of sowing, reaping, and compound return at work in our country's health care crisis?

2. How have you seen the principle of sowing, reaping, and compound return at work in your life?

3. What kind of future *health harvest* would you like to reap? When you think about your body stewardship, what is some good seed you could begin sowing?

ENJOY...a New You!

We are not victims of random chance, as a sovereign God is in control and has instituted a cause and effect principle for our benefit!

Sowing with you,

I Was Created To Move, Not To Be Sedentary.

ENGAGE...a New Day

Stewardship, husbandry, and dominion are the roles God created me to exercise on the earth. He created me with both the intellect and the physiology to fulfill these roles. While my God-given intellect may cause me to develop efficiencies and conveniences, I have not been created for or called to a pursuit of comfort and ease.

DAY 22

ELEVATE…with God's Word

So God created man in his own image, in the image of God he created him; male and female he created them. And God blessed them. And God said to them, "Be fruitful and multiply and fill the earth and subdue it, and have dominion over the fish of the sea and over the birds of the heavens and over every living thing that moves on the earth."

—Genesis 1:27–28

Six days you shall labor, and do all your work.

—Exodus 20:9

She looks well to the ways of her household and does not eat the bread of idleness.

—Proverbs 31:27

In all toil there is profit, but mere talk tends only to poverty.

—Proverbs 14:23

And we urge you, brothers, admonish the idle, encourage the fainthearted, help the weak, be patient with them all.

—1 Thessalonians 5:14

For you yourselves know how you ought to imitate us, because we were not idle when we were with you,

—2 Thessalonians 3:7

And he said, 'I will do this: I will tear down my barns and build larger ones, and there I will store all my grain and my goods. And I will say to my soul, "Soul, you have ample goods laid up for many years; relax, eat, drink, be merry."' But God said to him, 'Fool! This night your soul is required of you, and the things you have prepared, whose will they be?'

—Luke 12:18–20

EXCHANGE…with David Bush

The Disney/Pixar movie *Wall-E* foreshadows a future where our headlong pursuit of technology, ease, and convenience creates a society of sedentary and obese citizens who are transported everywhere. They expend little energy to lift a thing thanks to automation and voice command robotics.

While this may seem to be an exaggerated perspective of our future, in many ways we are creating just this kind of world. Our human ingenuity has developed lighter, more flexible, and more durable materials for construction, fashion, and mobility that have transformed our daily life. Resistance has largely been removed from our normal routines, and the need and opportunity to exert effort to transport ourselves from one place to another is disappearing. Coming soon are autonomous/driverless cars that will remove the need to press an accelerator or brake pedal, turn a wheel, or even crane our necks to view traffic.

There is nothing innately wrong with this progress, as the unique human capacity to mold our environment to suit our needs and desires is actually a demonstration of the dominion God commanded us to exercise. We are reflecting our Creator when we create more efficient and productive ways of accomplishing our tasks. God is glorified when we use our capacity as image-bearers to solve a problem brought on by the fall.

I believe the ultimate expression of productivity will be experienced by those living in the Millennial Kingdom, when Jesus is reigning on the earth. Likewise, the new heaven and earth will not represent an eternity of ease and sedentary pursuits, but of maximized productivity and joy. Citizens of heaven will be perfectly aligned with their Savior, their fellow citizens, and their purposeful and life-giving vocations.

As wonderful as our intellectual superiority over the rest of creation is, we might actually learn something from the animal kingdom when it comes to our physical stewardship. Even King Solomon, whose God-given intellect ushered in major advancements in discovery and productivity, saw the necessity of labor and industriousness as illustrated in the life of an ant in Proverbs 6:6–11 (ESV):

Go to the ant, O sluggard; consider her ways, and be wise.

Without having any chief, officer, or ruler, she prepares her bread in summer

and gathers her food in harvest. How long will you lie there, O sluggard?

When will you arise from your sleep? A little sleep, a little slumber,

a little folding of the hands to rest, and poverty will come upon you like a robber, and want like an armed man.

While it is possible today to be sedentary and productive thanks to technology, we are ultimately making withdrawals from our future productivity when we ignore our physical health.

The fact is, God created physiological realities that are part of our lives as well as the spiritual, emotional, and intellectual. We decry the waste of intellectual capital when we see people fritter away their time and capacity on mindless pursuits. But our physical bodies operate under the laws of use it or lose it as well.

Most people today will need to actively pursue opportunities for cardiovascular stress and muscle maintenance and development. Our daily regimens no longer supply most people with sufficient opportunities to place our bodies under the physical stress necessary to build a body that will serve us well over a lifetime.

While it is not necessary to join a gym or fitness center to be healthy, it is at facilities like these that we can easily and safely replicate the physical demands that, until the last 30+ years, used to be a part of daily life.

It is a blessing to live in an age when dangerous physical

work and daily toil for a subsistence lifestyle are largely a thing of the past. Our advancements and labor-saving devices, however, have not altered God's design and purpose for our physical existence. We are still created to move, and God's structuring of our workweek, which incorporates six days of engagement for each Sabbath, remains a timeless testimony to this fact. When you think of God's blessings, I hope you can view the ability to engage in vigorous activity as a manifestation of this, rather than a life that is increasingly easy, comfortable, and convenient.

EXPLORE…a Fresh Start

1. How has the vocation you are presently engaged in changed over the years to make it less physically taxing?

2. Will the physical demands of your current job and lifestyle be sufficient to sustain and build a healthy physical body?

3. Can you think of Scriptures that speak of people who are wealthy, overfed, and pursuing a life of ease and comfort? Does Scripture praise these people for their success and resourcefulness or warn and condemn them?

ENJOY…a New You!

God has given, as a gift to us, bodies that can achieve and produce at an amazing level. He takes pleasure in seeing us fully function as designed!

Staying as active as I can for as long as I can,

Though My Physical Body Will Ultimately Deteriorate And Die Because Of Sin, I Have The Promise Of A New, Perfect Body That Will Be Like Jesus' Resurrected Body.

ENGAGE...a New Day

The great hope of every Christian is the promise that Jesus will *make all things new*. This promise includes a new heaven and earth in which God again can enjoy intimacy with His creation, soil that fully cooperates with humanity's stewardship, a new proximity to Jesus that delights and provokes worship, and a new, imperishable body. My pursuit of transformation into the likeness of Christ should, therefore, include this physical reality in addition to the character qualities I am to increasingly exhibit.

DAY 23

ELEVATE...with God's Word

Beloved, we are God's children now, and what we will be has not yet appeared; but we know that when he appears we shall be like him, because we shall see him as he is.

—1 John 3:2

But our citizenship is in heaven, and from it we await a Savior, the Lord Jesus Christ, who will transform our lowly body to be like his glorious body, by the power that enables him even to subject all things to himself.

—Philippians 3:20–21

Behold! I tell you a mystery. We shall not all sleep, but we shall all be changed, in a moment, in the twinkling of an eye, at the last trumpet. For the trumpet will sound, and the dead will be raised imperishable, and we shall be changed. For this perishable body must put on the imperishable, and this mortal body must put on immortality.

—1 Corinthians 15:51–53

EXCHANGE…with David Bush

The financial crisis of 2008-2009 and the current burden of student debt shared by so many younger families has created a revitalized market for rentals. The prospect of home ownership has been postponed or has disappeared for a large number of people, giving rise to a growing number of landlords.

With the swelling number of renters has come a number of landlord services and websites, some dedicated to documenting the kind of rental nightmares every landlord wants to avoid. I happened upon an egregious example recently:

After losing his job, a renter in Chicago went months without paying his rent. When the landlord tried to evict the man, he filed for multiple extensions and drew out the legal process for months. The landlord was eventually given control of the apartment, but not until he'd endured numerous court appearances and eight months of nonpayment.

Sadly, this landlord's nightmare had only begun. The new tenants of the apartment noticed a strange odor and complained to management. Nothing the landlord did could get rid of the smell. Carpet cleaning, new HVAC filters, and more were to no avail. After all avenues had been exhausted, the property manager noticed a slight discoloration on the walls. When he poked a few holes through the drywall, maggots crawled out.

Further inspection revealed that the disgruntled evicted tenant, before leaving the unit, had hidden packages of raw meat behind the walls throughout the apartment. All the drywall and insulation in the apartment and the surrounding units had to be replaced to get rid of the unbearable stench.[1]

The episode described above is, obviously, a singularly horrific landlord experience. Yet it illustrates a truth we all know exists: whether it is homes, apartments, cars, jet skis or ice skates, people (I'm sure you are the exception) often treat rentals with less care and caution than they do their own property.

Here's where we need to be careful as Christians. Most of us cling to the glorious hope of all believers that we will ultimately receive new, imperishable bodies that will not experience decay and death. Jesus and the apostles spoke repeatedly of this, and Jesus' resurrected body is offered as an example of what that physical body will be like.

With our future secure in this incredible promise, it would be easy to experience growing contempt for our current bodies, especially as they age and deteriorate. If we're not careful, we can begin to think of them as nothing more than a temporary shell to be cast off like a butterfly's chrysalis.

In short, we are all tempted to treat our current bodies like a rental.

David Mathis, Pastor of Cities Church in Minneapolis, MN, and Executive Editor at *Desiring God* reminds us in a recent blog:

The creative brilliance and glory of God's design in the human body will not be discarded at Christ's second coming.

Our future is embodied. Faithful Christian theology does not diminish the importance of our bodies, but heightens it—from God's creative design, to his ongoing affirmation, to his promise to raise them, to his calling to use them.[2]

Our bodies will degrade and eventually die. But this in no way marginalizes them. Like all animate and inanimate things that are crying out for redemption, our calling is to show forth the promise of redeemed perfection in our present state.

Will our tongues be completely redeemed at some future time? How about our relationships? Will we see a new heaven and a new earth? If we believe Scripture affirms this, what is our logical response? Maximize our profanity now while we can…destroy our relationships while that remains a possibility…pollute the earth? After all, everything gets redeemed in the end!

While these ludicrous responses to God's future promises may seem over the top, we need to make sure the certainty of new physical bodies does not create in us a dismissive attitude toward the ones God has entrusted us with now. While we won't attain perfection in our present state, our pursuit of Christlikeness should be inspired by what we know of our future physical perfection.

Jesus' resurrected body is the down payment for the glorified bodies we are promised. Glorifying God now with our bodies provides a foretaste of what we will receive in the future.

EXPLORE...a Fresh Start

1. Do you have a rental horror story of your own?

2. From the gospel accounts, what do we know about Jesus' resurrected body?

3. What changes do you anticipate will be present in your new, glorified body? What is within your power to do now to align yourself with that future reality?

ENJOY...a New You!

God desires to use all of who we are to declare that He is doing a redemptive work in His creation! In Christ, we have the promise of a new, completely redeemed body!

Looking forward with you to the new model,

---

1. Anne McMillin, *When Renting Goes Wrong: 6 Tenant Horror Stories*, Avail.com, April 3, 2019, https://www.avail.co/education/articles/when-renting-goes-wrong-6-tenant-horror-stories

2. David Mathis, *Do You Exercise for the Wrong Reasons?*, DesiringGod.org, January 26, 2017, https://www.desiringgod.org/articles/do-you-exercise-for-the-wrong-reasons

The Gospel That Redeemed My Spirit Is The Same Gospel That Is At Work Redeeming My Relationships, My Finances, My Tongue, My Physical Body And Everything Else Of Consequence In My Life.

ENGAGE...a New Day

The power of the gospel does not end at my salvation. Starting with our spirits, the gospel continues to do its work redeeming every aspect of my life. I never grow out of the gospel; instead I grow up and into the transforming power of the gospel throughout my walk with Christ.

DAY 24

ELEVATE...with God's Word

For the grace of God has appeared, bringing salvation for all people, training us to renounce ungodliness and worldly passions, and to live self-controlled, upright, and godly lives in the present age, waiting for our blessed hope, the appearing of the glory of our great God and Savior Jesus Christ, who gave himself for us to redeem us from all lawlessness and to purify for himself a people for his own possession who are zealous for good works.

—Titus 2:11–14

And I am sure of this, that he who began a good work in you will bring it to completion at the day of Jesus Christ.

—Philippians 1:6

For we know that the whole creation has been groaning together in the pains of childbirth until now. And not only the creation, but we ourselves, who have the firstfruits of the Spirit, groan inwardly as we wait eagerly for adoption as sons, the redemption of our bodies.

—Romans 8:22–23

EXCHANGE…with David Bush

Chip and Joanna Gaines have become wildly popular because of their ability to take forsaken real estate and transform them into inviting, livable homes. Like the legions of *house flippers* who have sought to follow their example and spin gold from flax, the Gaineses continue to take on what often appears to be a questionable property renovation with obvious flaws only to painstakingly transform it into something of beauty for the owners.

Viewers of their show, *Fixer Upper,* watch the transformation take place step by step, building to the climactic "Big Reveal" where the owners return to the formerly dilapidated residence to see the final result of the transformative work Chip and Joanna have done.

What the Gaineses accomplish for real estate in Waco, Texas, is a picture of what the Holy Spirit is attempting to do with those who belong to Jesus.

He *buys our house* when we come to faith in Christ, and the Holy Spirit redeems our spirits. The ravages of sin have made this a questionable investment, to be sure, but God sees the potential of our lives in Christ. His glory is compounded by the extent of the transformative work He needs to accomplish.

With the title deed to our lives in His possession, the Holy Spirit moves from the redemption He's brought to our spirits to beginning the lifelong redemptive work He seeks to accomplish. This transformative work is intended to impact our finances, relationships, language, thinking, entertainment choices, and physical bodies. Every aspect of our lives participates in this holistic makeover. The climax of this sanctifying work is a *Big Reveal* where the cumulative work we have allowed the Holy Spirit to accomplish in us is revealed to men and angels to the glory of God.

We can bring glory to God in the present tense by cooperating fully with the sanctifying work the Spirit is seeking to do in our bodies. We can present to the world a picture of what our fully redeemed bodies will look like.

The gospel's redemptive power is fueled by our humble response to God's grace, the perfection of His love, our righteous standing in Christ, His persevering forgiveness of our shortcomings, and His promise to complete His work in us. Living daily in the reality of these gospel truths creates momentum in our transformation. Praise God, He has given us all we need to accomplish His purposes in our lives!

Notes:

EXPLORE...a Fresh Start

1. How have you seen the Holy Spirit do a transforming and sanctifying work regarding your language, finances, relationships and media choices?

2. Would someone encountering your physical body come away with the impression it was being progressively sanctified?

3. What aspect of the gospel do you need to understand or *own* more fully to see greater progress in your sanctification?

ENJOY...a New You!

God desires to use all of who we are to declare that He is doing a redemptive work in His creation!

Redeeming today and its opportunities by God's grace,

God Has Equipped All Believers With Gifts He Intends To Be Used For The Benefit Of The Body Of Christ, The Church. My Health Directly Impacts My Ability To Be Effective In Using These Gifts And Serving Others In The Church.

ENGAGE...a New Day

God has created the physical and spiritual aspects of my being. God intends to use both as His primary means of displaying the gospel at work. Stewarding my physical health is a tangible means of not only serving my nuclear family, but also of remaining available to serve my spiritual family with my unique gifts.

ELEVATE...with God's Word

As each has received a gift, use it to serve one another, as good stewards of God's varied grace

—1 Peter 4:10

Now there are varieties of gifts, but the same Spirit; and there are varieties of service, but the same Lord; and there are varieties of activities, but it is the same God who empowers them all in everyone. To each is given the manifestation of the Spirit for the common good...But as it is, God arranged the members in the body, each one of them, as he chose. If all were a single member, where would the body be?

—1 Corinthians 12:4–7, 18

Rather, speaking the truth in love, we are to grow up in every way into him who is the head, into Christ, from whom the whole body, joined and held together by every joint with which it is equipped, when each part is working properly, makes the body grow so that it builds itself up in love.

—Ephesians 4:15–16

Having gifts that differ according to the grace given to us, let us use them: if prophecy, in proportion to our faith; if service, in our serving; the one who teaches, in his teaching; the one who exhorts, in his exhortation; the one who contributes, in generosity; the one who leads, with zeal; the one who does acts of mercy, with cheerfulness...Do not be slothful in zeal, be fervent in spirit, serve the Lord.

—Romans 12:6–8, 11

EXCHANGE...with David Bush

Do you view yourself as necessary for the health of your church? Scripture makes it clear that our participation in the life of the body of Christ is critical and orchestrated by the Spirit of God. The Apostle Paul's symbolic use of the human body drives this point home. No physical body can function properly when even one part is weak.

A person attending church today will often hear about the many ways their wants and needs can be met by various programs and services offered. We can easily begin to view ourselves as consumers who are motivated by how comprehensively the church meets the perceived needs of our families.

While this approach undoubtedly fosters the numerical growth of the church, it does not follow the biblical model where each member seeks how to best serve others in the body with their set of Spirit-empowered gifts. This consumer-driven approach also gives rise to the "20% Rule"—where twenty percent of the church (a subset of the "members") serve the eighty percent ("regular attenders").

This consumer mindset, and the lack of faithful servers it produces, is compounded by the poor physical condition of many in the body of Christ. Too many saints with indispensable spiritual gifts are sidelined because they do not possess the physical vitality to remain engaged. Frequent illnesses fostered by chronic illnesses keep people on the sidelines instead of on the playing field.

In most churches I've been involved with, a critical source of volunteer help comes from the retirees in the congregation. In these cases, the faithful body stewardship of seniors proves to be a great blessing to the church. Those who have not stewarded their health well, however, can become an unintentional drain on its resources.

I don't want to be unkind, and I want to affirm that the church should be available to serve those who have legitimate physical and emotional needs. But I also feel compelled to say that energy and resources that could be spent reaching our communities and world for Christ are often used on members of the body whose lifestyle decisions have placed them in a position of perpetual need.

How many of the requests on our prayer lists are from

individuals asking for divine intervention that will lessen the consequences of sedentary and undisciplined lifestyles? How many church resources are expended so that members of the body are insulated from the difficult work of personal transformation by the Spirit?

The Holy Spirit has given all members of the body gifts He intends to be employed for the benefit of all. No member is more important, and no gift is more significant than another. We all need each other. Are you willing to steward your physical body in a way that ensures you will be available to make the contributions to the body the Spirit desires? We're all depending on you!

Notes:

EXPLORE...a Fresh Start

1. Have you ever (perhaps with the help of a gifting assessment of some kind) identified your spiritual gift(s)?

2. How might your ability to steward these be impacted by your level of health?

3. Have you ever considered the responsibility you have to the Body of Christ to employ your spiritual gift(s) regularly and skillfully? Is your church suffering in some way because you are unwilling or unable to contribute your gift?

ENJOY...a New You!

There are many in your church body who want and need your contributions. Your good body stewardship is a tangible service to them!

Constantly reminded that we need each other,

As An Ambassador For Christ, I Am Called
To Represent His Transforming Work In My Life
And To Remove Barriers To Faith In Others
Who Are Observing My Life.

ENGAGE...a New Day

Followers of Jesus do not opt into ambassadorship. I am either a good ambassador or a poor ambassador. I represent Christ in all aspects of my life, and my physical body will be the first thing people see before they have a chance to hear my story or before my character, values, and beliefs are revealed.

DAY 26

ELEVATE...with God's Word

Therefore, we are ambassadors for Christ, God making his appeal through us. We implore you on behalf of Christ, be reconciled to God.

—2 Corinthians 5:20

Keep your conduct among the Gentiles honorable, so that when they speak against you as evildoers, they may see your good deeds and glorify God on the day of visitation.

—1 Peter 2:12

But take care that this right of yours does not somehow become a stumbling block to the weak…So, whether you eat or drink, or whatever you do, do all to the glory of God. Give no offense to Jews or to Greeks or to the church of God, just as I try to please everyone in everything I do, not seeking my own advantage, but that of many, that they may be saved.

—1 Corinthians 8:9; 10:31–33

EXCHANGE…with David Bush

I had the opportunity recently to have lunch with a couple who had been impacted by the body stewardship ministry I lead. Together they had lost over 130 pounds of excess weight and were both experiencing a new lease on life. Both were committed Christians who served in their local church and in vocational ministry. The husband had nearly died of a massive heart attack a couple of years previously.

During our conversation, he shared with me a comment a friend had made to him well into his physical transformation. "You must be excited," this well-meaning individual told him. "Now you will have more credibility in your ministry." At the time, this comment caught him off guard. He had assumed those evaluating his life would look at his commitment to his wife, the way he raised his children, and the millions of dollars he'd helped raise for a gospel-based social needs ministry in our community as sufficient evidence that his walk with Christ was genuine. What he learned that day was a hard, perhaps unfair reality that every ambassador of Jesus will have to confront: People you encounter will observe—and often arrive at conclusions—based on your visible physical state. Oftentimes this is before someone can see the spiritual, relational, and emotional healing, growth, and transformation the Holy Spirit is working in your life.

Evaluating people's effectiveness in the Kingdom based on their physical fitness alone is a foolish exercise. There are many factors at work in the physiology of people, including genetic and hormonal factors that may be out of their control. It's also true that those who appear physically disciplined could be harboring hidden sin and dysfunction in other areas of their lives.

The unavoidable fact remains that we are all considered ambassadors; the question is whether we're good ambassadors or poor ambassadors. If we are publicly professing our faith in Christ (and shouldn't that include all of us?), we open the door to the likelihood that others will, in some way, be evaluating our lives to see in what ways our behavior aligns with the standard we profess to follow. Do we appear to be walking in freedom and newness of life? Do we appear to have rejected the excesses of an undisciplined life? Are we living counter-culturally?

Like the Apostle Paul, may we all commit to removing all stumbling blocks and offenses, save the cross, so that the reality of Christ's transforming power is the greatest impression we make.

Notes:

EXPLORE…a Fresh Start

1. What do you think the difference is between exercising discernment and making invalid judgments?

2. Can you think of examples where Jesus or Scripture writers affirmed the appropriateness of evaluating conduct and arriving at conclusions? (See Matthew 12:33; James 2:18)

3. Can you think of changes in your behavior or appearance that might improve your ambassadorship?

4. Where might a Christian draw the line in their pursuit of cultural relevance in the name of better ambassadorship?

ENJOY...a New You!

God has entrusted to us (vessels of clay) the privilege and responsibility of accurately representing Him to others. What a challenge!

Your fellow Ambassador,

As A Steward Of All God Has Entrusted To Me, I Guard And Invest In One Of His Greatest Trusts, My Physical Body, So I Can Provide Him The Greatest Possible Return On Investment.

ENGAGE...a New Day

While finances are a central aspect of any conversation about biblical stewardship, this is by no means the only area of personal management with which God is concerned. My physical body is the greatest resource I have been given, as it impacts my ability to steward everything else with which God entrusts me.

ELEVATE...with God's Word

Moreover, it is required of stewards that they be found faithful.

—1 Corinthians 4:2

For to everyone who has will more be given, and he will have an abundance. But from the one who has not, even what he has will be taken away

—Matthew 25:29

For no one ever hated his own flesh, but nourishes and cherishes it, just as Christ does the church…

—Ephesians 5:29

Do you not know that in a race all the runners run, but only one receives the prize? So run that you may obtain it. Every athlete exercises self-control in all things. They do it to receive a perishable wreath, but we an imperishable.

—1 Corinthians 9:24–25

EXCHANGE…with David Bush

Dave Ramsey has helped many in the church transform their financial situations by applying biblical principles to how they handle the monetary resources entrusted to them. "Live like no one else—so that someday you can live and *give* like no one else," has been his mantra.[1] Those willing to respond in compliance have found themselves more available to follow the Lord's leading free from the bondage of consumer debt.

One of the challenges facing anyone who wants to be a faithful financial steward is the shortsightedness and invulnerability of youth. When we are young, retirement seems an eternity away, and it is easy to think we'll have decades to worry about our future nest egg. *What difference can saving a small amount each month make at this point in my life?* we ask as irresistible purchases call for our resources. But in postponing our commitment to save for the future, we miss out on years of compounding that will fortify our future financial freedom.

Of course, our stewardship involves far more than our financial resources. God has entrusted each of us with relationships, skills, talents, and opportunities that are potential catalysts to expand the reach of the gospel. Everyone is not responsible for the same universal stewardship, as He gives each of us a unique combination of opportunities. Not everyone will be married, have children, be responsible for employees, lead a church, or hold political office. But all of us have financial resources we're expected to steward for the benefit of the One who owns everything.

We all have physical bodies as well, representing perhaps the most significant area of stewardship for which we are responsible. Without a vital and functioning physical body, many of the other things God has entrusted to us can become compromised, including our finances.

Sadly, the same barriers that exist to faithful financial stewardship are present in our body stewardship. In our youth, the tendency is to see ourselves as indestructible, and investments in good nutrition and building a strong physical foundation are often not prioritized. Greater physical resiliency and a revved up metabolism compensate for poor eating choices and a lack of vigorous activity in this early season of life. The result: a shaky foundation for future vitality.

The latter years of our lives provide possibly the greatest potential for impacting the Kingdom of God through our accumulated wisdom, resources, experience, and connections. We can leverage all these things for the sake of the gospel *if we are alive and possess the physical vitality necessary to steward them well.* A faithful steward will look into the future and establish a lifestyle that provides the best path possible to remain healthy, vital, and engaged for as long as possible.

A common reality today is the person nearing retirement who realizes they don't have enough money to retire or even live independently. There are not enough years remaining to save and invest, and the realization hits that they should have made changes to their lifestyle many years previously that would have allowed for adequate savings to provide financial security. A financial windfall is the only thing that can change a grim financial picture. The only alternative is to continue working as long as is physically possible.

This undesirable scenario is playing itself out for many in the physical arena of life today as well. It is often in their 60s that people approach a wellness coach looking to remedy decades of neglect. While there are things that can be done to lessen the damage and make improvements, the best time to have taken an interest in physical stewardship was in their youth, when it did not seem important or relevant.

Whether you are young or old, today is the day to take seriously the stewardship of your body. Whether you have but a few years or a lifetime ahead of you, your faithful stewardship of your physical resources will pay dividends in your spiritual vitality and your ability to engage a world in need of the gospel.

EXPLORE...a Fresh Start

1. Have you ever thought much about stewardship outside of the financial realm?

2. In the Parable of the Talents (Matthew 25:14–30), Jesus is more concerned with the motive and willingness to steward what a person is entrusted with as opposed to the gross return. How do you see this principle applying to our stewardship of our physical capacity?

3. What can you pursue now in the area of fitness and nutrition that can improve your stewardship of your most valuable asset—your physical body?

4. Jesus and Paul both make it clear there are heavenly rewards for those who steward well the resources they are given. Do you believe this is true? Do you think the rewards offered are worth the cost of sacrificial living in your temporal life? If not, what does this say about your view of God's generosity?

ENJOY...a New You!

In your body stewardship, God has given you an amazing responsibility with eternal significance!

Investing with you in Kingdom impact,

1. Dave Ramsey, *Tired of Keeping Up with the Joneses?*, Daveramsey.com (blog), June 19, 2019, https://www.daveramsey.com/blog/tired-of-keeping-up-with-the-joneses.

Cooperating With The Spirit's Transformative Work In My Life And Others' Lives Will Require Me To Be Sensitive And Honest About Snares And Obstacles To Growth.

ENGAGE...a New Day

Loving fellow believers and helping them grow in body stewardship may involve telling them the truth in love. It will also sometimes mean giving up rights in the area of food and drink for their benefit.

DAY 28

ELEVATE...with God's Word

Let the word of Christ dwell in you richly, teaching and admonishing one another in all wisdom, singing psalms and hymns and spiritual songs, with thankfulness in your hearts to God.

—Colossians 3:16

Rather, speaking the truth in love, we are to grow up in every way into him who is the head, into Christ, from whom the whole body, joined and held together by every joint with which it is equipped, when each part is working properly, makes the body grow so that it builds itself up in love.

—Ephesians 4:15–16

"All things are lawful for me," but not all things are helpful. "All things are lawful for me," but I will not be dominated by anything.

—1 Corinthians 6:12

Therefore, if food makes my brother stumble, I will never eat meat, lest I make my brother stumble.

—1 Corinthians 8:13

Therefore let us not pass judgment on one another any longer, but rather decide never to put a stumbling block or hindrance in the way of a brother…For if your brother is grieved by what you eat, you are no longer walking in love…By what you eat, do not destroy the one for whom Christ died…Do not, for the sake of food, destroy the work of God. Everything is indeed clean, but it is wrong for anyone to make another stumble by what he eats.

—Romans 14:13,15,20

EXCHANGE…with David Bush

I was disturbed to read recently about a church that was opening up a taproom in their Welcome Center. A selection of domestic and imported beers would join with traditional coffee offerings in welcoming parishioners to worship. In its desire to be edgy and relevant to its hipster target, it seemed that this church was yielding to a worldly marketing scheme as well as being grossly insensitive to those who struggle with an addiction to alcohol.

Honestly, though, most churches are already in the habit of offering foods that present a stumbling block to many members of the body. Most churches I visit provide refreshments that are highly processed and loaded with sugar. What is perceived as hospitality fuels an addiction for many in the church every bit as real and debilitating as drugs and alcohol.

I was reminded of this recently when an attendee at one of our *Fit For The King* workshops related her story of confession to her small group Bible study. Convicted of an addiction to sugar and highly processed carbohydrates, she came clean with her peers. "Oh, no dear," they protested, "you're not an addict!" It became necessary to detail her emotional and physical bondage before they were willing to accept the reality of her ordeal and agree they needed to go in a different direction in the area of refreshments.

Building up, encouraging, and admonishing a brother or sister in Christ in need of help is a risky but biblical responsibility we have in the church. I assure you that those in the throes of a food addiction are not likely to respond well to direct confrontation outside of a relationship that has already displayed love, trust, and mutual respect. Personal examples of how your life has been positively impacted by good body stewardship will likely be more effective than correction that can easily be interpreted as condemnation.

Because we love people, however, it will at times be necessary to have honest discussions about sensitive topics. Bathing these conversations in prayer, and approaching them with both truth and grace, allows the healing power of the gospel to shine into strongholds that are longing for redemption.

Notes:

EXPLORE...a Fresh Start

1. Have you ever attempted to bring correction into the life of a fellow believer? How was it received?

2. Of what importance is relationship when confrontation becomes necessary?

3. Is your church a safe place or a stumbling block to the food/sugar addict (or diabetics or those not at a healthy weight)? What changes could be made to balance hospitality with not causing a brother to stumble?

ENJOY...a New You!

We have the opportunity each week to assist in the work and growth God is doing in the lives of others in the body of Christ.

Trying, with you, to speak the truth in love,

Transformation Is Not A Solo Project.

ENGAGE...a New Day

No aspect of our growth in Christ is intended to be routinely pursued in isolation. Fellowship, encouragement, and accountability are necessary by design. Jesus Himself modeled the way transformation takes place in His relationship with His disciples, and the church grows out of that model.

ELEVATE...with God's Word

If one member suffers, all suffer together; if one member is honored, all rejoice together. Now you are the body of Christ and individually members of it.

—1 Corinthians 12:26–27

Therefore, confess your sins to one another and pray for one another, that you may be healed. The prayer of a righteous person has great power as it is working.

—James 5:16

And we urge you, brothers, admonish the idle, encourage the fainthearted, help the weak, be patient with them all.

—1 Thessalonians 5:14

Iron sharpens iron, and one man sharpens another.

—Proverbs 27:17

So we, though many, are one body in Christ, and individually members one of another.

—Romans 12:5

Bear one another's burdens, and so fulfill the law of Christ.

—Galatians 6:2

EXCHANGE…with David Bush

The health club has always been a place I've found to be fruitful in sharing my faith with other people. Serving as a pastor for over twenty years, I've had to seek out opportunities to rub shoulders with people who don't know Jesus, and the camaraderie present in many fitness centers has allowed me to have a ministry there.

But I've noticed a trend in fitness clubs over the past several years. With advancing technology, an increasing number of club members are retreating into their own worlds through podcasts, Spotify and iTunes playlists, and social media chatter. Several times I've been embarrassed when I began conversations with others who had tuned out.

This development tends to feed a negative image among many who cast a wary eye at gym culture. Already viewed by some as a narcissistic and selfish pursuit, this kind of isolationism is one more reason to reject our culture's predominant choice for exercise.

Interestingly, this same tendency toward isolationism is present in the church. With so many resources available for personal study, the benefits of life-on-life discipleship are sometimes lost. The fact is, it's hard to grow alone. That's why our flesh and Satan seek to isolate us. Conversely, the Spirit incorporates us into loving, encouraging, and accountable relationships.

Jesus sets the example for us. In the midst of broader contact with dozens of disciples, Jesus focuses his attention on twelve and even more intentionally on three or four. Through his close interactions, we see dramatic growth and maturity in just a matter of years. With the filling of the Holy Spirit at Pentecost, these ordinary men were ready for substantive ministry.

It is normal for us to gather in one-on-one and group discipleship settings as we grow in our faith. Why should it be any different in this critical area of physical transformation, where encouragement, instruction, and accountability are sorely needed? While resources for the church in the area of body stewardship are lacking, this is an area experiencing growth. *Fit For the King* has a number of resources that could be used to assist in the area of body care at *www.fit4theking.net.*

For those with a bent toward an excessive emphasis on exercise and diet, a supportive community of faith might be just the accountability factor needed to avoid imbalance in this area.

While the health club will continue to represent a great opportunity for exercise and outreach, what many in the body of Christ need is an encouraging and supportive place to pursue physical transformation. It has been encouraging to see participants in *Fit For the King* group fitness classes grow in their understanding of holistic discipleship through their involvement in corporate exercise centered on Scripture. Growing in body stewardship is just another aspect of discipleship that is intended to include the encouragement, admonition, and accountability that is necessary for our spiritual growth.

With all the laughter, sharing, and encouragement present, no one wants to put in their earbuds!

EXPLORE...a Fresh Start

1. How have you benefited from one-on-one or small group discipleship in the past?

2. Have you seen victories over areas of bondage or unbiblical thinking because of this kind of community and accountability?

3. If you need help, encouragement, and support to become more physically available, would it make sense to enlist the help of others?

4. If you're in a health rut, would it make more sense to ask for assistance from another who is struggling or someone who seems to have achieved a healthy balance in their exercise and eating patterns?

5. If you need help, are you humble enough to ask for help?

ENJOY...a New You!

God doesn't want you to go it alone in your pursuit of good body care or any other area of your sanctification. He wants to use you in the lives of others as well!

Locking arms with you in pursuit of the prize,

Personal And Corporate Revival Demands A Body That Can Engage In The Spiritual Disciplines.

ENGAGE...a New Day

The spiritual disciplines that accompany revival include prayer, fasting, and meditation on God's Word. When I discipline my body, I remove spiritual barriers to fully cooperate with the Holy Spirit's work of renewal.

ELEVATE...with God's Word

But I discipline my body and keep it under control, lest after preaching to others I myself should be disqualified.

—1 Corinthians 9:27

And rising very early in the morning, while it was still dark, he departed and went out to a desolate place, and there he prayed.

—Mark 1:35

And when you fast, do not look gloomy like the hypocrites, for they disfigure their faces that their fasting may be seen by others. Truly, I say to you, they have received their reward. But when you fast, anoint your head and wash your face, that your fasting may not be seen by others but by your Father who is in secret. And your Father who sees in secret will reward you.

—Matthew 6:16–18

But I, brothers, could not address you as spiritual people, but as people of the flesh, as infants in Christ. I fed you with milk, not solid food, for you were not ready for it. And even now you are not yet ready

—1 Corinthians 3:1–2

if my people who are called by my name humble themselves, and pray and seek my face and turn from their wicked ways, then I will hear from heaven and will forgive their sin and heal their land.

—2 Chronicles 7:14

…for God gave us a spirit not of fear but of power and love and self-control.

—2 Timothy 1:7

EXCHANGE…with David Bush

Those surveying the American landscape know something is desperately wrong. Our society is in moral freefall, and broad speculation exists as to how long our country can endure in its present form. The church, God's institution on earth tasked with calling people and governments to repentance, seems impotent in the face of such an overwhelming task. If confronted, the powerful forces of government and the media seem increasingly intolerant of moral absolutes, leaving many to wonder when persecution of the church will increase.

Those interpreting the signs of the times see two options as most likely: ramped up persecution of the church (both corporately and individually), or an outbreak of revival in our land. Some would say both are probable and, perhaps, necessary. One thing most agree upon: Revival is the last best chance our country has to survive.

I have heard people pray for revival for years, and I have personally joined in the chorus. "Lord, bring revival to our land," is the common refrain. A promise to the nation of Israel in 2 Chronicles 7:14 has become an inspiration for many, as it contains a template for spiritual renewal directed at those who belong to God. While few would argue revival is a work initiated by God's Spirit, what responsibility do we have in God-initiated societal transformation? What, if any, physiological factors are inherent in a widespread movement of the Holy Spirit?

Pastor Glenn Meldrum of In His Presence Ministries says this:

Revival is the sovereign activity of God. No one can force His hand to act, or else He would not be the Almighty. Yet the Lord has chosen to place responsibility for revival in the hands of men. This is the great mystery of revival: the Lord sovereignly moves and yet acts in accordance with the prayers of His people.

For revival to come, we must comprehend that in and of ourselves, we can do nothing. Yet, our responsibility is real. This means that a cooperative effort between God and man takes place for the Spirit to be poured out. God has given us the privilege of pursuing revival through those means He has established in His written Word. The Spirit moves the hearts of men to move the heart of God—a mystery indeed. Revival is always a move of the Spirit that produces repentance and personal holiness. It cannot be otherwise.[1]

If we have a responsibility in the sovereign work of revival, it would seem to be the work of preparing ourselves personally to invite the Lord's reviving work in our own lives, and repenting of anything His Spirit reveals is an impediment. Historically this has meant pursuing the spiritual disciplines of prayer, fasting, meditating on God's Word, and solitude. Those pursuing these disciplines will soon find how difficult they are to sustain, as well as how out of step they are with the current Christian subculture. For years, the momentum has been with church growth and relevancy, not personal discipleship, repentance, and countercultural living.

But if revival is the only option left to us to see our culture redeemed, it seems that a pursuit of this should stimulate our thinking and actions. This logical progression comes with the unsettling fact that any revival that impacts the church and culture begins in the lives of individuals. Derek Prince states,

All my greatest spiritual successes began by saying 'No' to myself, or words to that effect. Experience will teach you that if you want the real fire, the real power of God, the way you keep your body under [control] has a lot to do with it.[2]

While God is free to initiate revival any way He chooses, I wonder if He chooses not to act because of a church in America that is largely content, over-fed, over-prescribed, and sedentary. Previous generations that experienced revival did not have the same level of physical and spiritual deterioration our present generation has. Perhaps this is an area where repentance can begin. Can God override spiritual insensitivity fostered by our contemporary lifestyles? Of course He can.

But *will* He? What responsibility do we have to prepare ourselves, like John the Baptist's generation, for a great movement of the Lord? Would it also be wise to physically prepare yourself for a season of trial and testing amidst a culture that is more and more hostile to the things of God? The church could benefit from being more *battle hardened* with the likelihood of growing persecution .

Numerous gospel-centered motivations for pursuing good body stewardship have been presented over the past 30 days. Here is one final compelling motive to submit to the Spirit's transforming work in your life: The spiritual direction of our country may well hinge on the willingness of the church to rethink its current approach to body care, and to make the courageous and difficult decision to surrender itself to the pursuit of holistically holy living.

EXPLORE...a Fresh Start

1. If the Apostle Paul had to take action to discipline his body (1 Corinthians 9:27) in a culture more cooperative to healthy living than ours, what kinds of actions might we need to take in a culture brimming with unhealthy food options and labor-saving devices? Read 1 Corinthians 9 in its entirety and ask yourself: From what was Paul concerned about being disqualified?

2. Jesus talks about fasting in Matthew 6:16–18. After reading this passage, do you think He assumed this would be a regular part of His followers' experience or something only a few very devout people would pursue?

3. Do you agree with the statement "Apart from revival, America, as we've historically known her, is finished?"

4. If you don't agree, what, other than revival, holds the key to a better future? If you do agree, how are you positioning yourself to participate in personal and corporate revival?

ENJOY...a New You!

God has shown a willingness to bring revival to countries, including America, in the past. He uses surrendered members of His church to bring a spark of spiritual life to full flame. Our surrendered bodies and spirits are the kindling from which this flame grows.

Praying and preparing for revival,

1. Glenn Meldrum, *What Happens In Revival?*, Lifeaction.org, June 19, 2019, https://lifeaction.org/what-happens-in-revival/

2. Derek Prince, *Self-Discipline—Key To Revival and Spiritual Success,* christian-faith.com, June 19, 2019, https://www.christian-faith.com/self-discipline-key-to-revival-and-spiritual-success/

Notes:

Notes:

Notes:

Notes:

Bibliography

Bush, David
Fit for the King: Your Health and God's Purpose for Your Life.
Des Moines, IA: King of Kings Publishing, 2015.

Chapman, Gary
The Five Love Languages:
How To Express Heartfelt Commitment To Your Mate
Chicago,IL: Northfield Publishing, 1992.

DC Talk
Free At Last, *Luv is a Verb.*
Brentwood, TN: Forefront Records, 1992. CD.

Mathis, David
Do You Exercise for the Wrong Reasons?
DesiringGod.org; January 26, 2017
https://www.desiringgod.org/articles/do-you-exercise-for-the-wrong-reasons.

McMillin, Anne
When Renting Goes Wrong: 6 Tenant Horror Stories
Avail.com; April 3, 2019
https://www.avail.co/education/articles/when-renting-goes-wrong-6-tenant-horror-stories.

Meldrum, Glenn.
What Happens In Revival?
Lifeaction.org; June 19, 2019
https://lifeaction.org/what-happens-in-revival/

Prince, Derek.
Self-Discipline—Key To Revival and Spiritual Success
christian-faith.com; June 19, 2019
https://www.christian-faith.com/self-discipline-key-to-revival-and-spiritual-success/

Ramsey, Dave.
Tired of Keeping Up with the Joneses?
Daveramsey.com (blog); June 19, 2019,
https://www.daveramsey.com/blog/tired-of-keeping-up-with-the-joneses.

StoriesfromtheWell.org

Wikipedia. 2019.
Roy Riegels
Last edited 20 January 2019
https://en.wikipedia.org/wiki/Roy_Riegels.

....

About the Author: David Bush is a pastor, Christian artist and worship leader, speaker, and Founder of Fit For The King, a body stewardship ministry of Point of Light Ministries. David has previously authored **Fit For The King: Your Health and God's Purpose For Your Life.** He has been married to his wife Beth for over thirty years, and together they have four adult sons, two daughters in-law, and one granddaughter. Learn more about Fit For The King at ***www.fit4theking.net***

LOOKING FOR

Order these Practical and Gospel-Centered

I appeal to you therefore, brothers, by the mercies of God, to present your bodies as a living sacrifice, holy and acceptable to God, which is your spiritual worship. Do not be conformed to this world, but be transformed by the renewal of your mind, that by testing you may discern what is the will of God, what is good and acceptable and perfect.

—Romans 12:1–2 (ESV)

MORE?

Fit For The King

Resources On Body Stewardship

When it comes to the topic of health and fitness, we live in a culture of extremes. Some follow the path of least resistance, eating large and often. Others become obsessed with fitness and diet. In the midst of this tug of war, is it possible to find a biblically-informed balance? David Bush and Joe Tewell give personal stories, biblical insights and practical help for those caught up in our culture's dysfunctional relationship with food and fitness.

Our daily journal provides critical accountability and information that can assist you in a physical transformation. Plenty of room to document meals and record workouts combined with valuable information on nutrition, calorie content of foods, exchanges, etc. This one-stop resource is a game-changer for those pursuing body transformation.

Available at Amazon.com and fit4theking.net

Made in the USA
Coppell, TX
07 July 2020